The Parthian Coinage: (with Eight Plates.)

Percy Gardner

THE INTERNATIONAL

NUMISMATA ORIENTALIA.

THE ADVANCED ARTICLES HAVE BEEN UNDERTAKEN BY THE FOLLOWING CONTRIBUTORS:

DR. H. BLOCHMANN.   GENERAL A. CUNNINGHAM.   MR. RHYS DAVIDS.   SIR WALTER ELLIOT.   PROF. JULIUS EUTING.
DON PASCUAL DE GAYANGOS.   PROFESSOR GREGORIEF.   MR. F. W. MADDEN.   SIR ARTHUR PHAYRE.
MR. REGINALD S. POOLE.   MR. STANLEY L. POOLE.   M. F. DE SAULCY.   M. H. SAUVAIRE.
MR. EDWARD THOMAS.

THE PARTHIAN COINAGE.

(WITH EIGHT PLATES.)

BY

PERCY GARDNER, M.A.,

BRITISH MUSEUM; LATE FELLOW OF CHRIST'S COLLEGE, CAMBRIDGE; FOREIGN SECRETARY OF THE NUMISMATIC
SOCIETY OF LONDON.

LONDON:

TRÜBNER & CO., 57 AND 59, LUDGATE HILL.

1877.

1·0313
.699
.37₈

.378

HERTFORD:
PRINTED BY STEPHEN AUSTIN AND SONS.

TABLE OF CONTENTS.

[1] Called, by a misprint, in the text Artabanus IV.

626100

iv   TABLE OF CONTENTS.

THE PARTHIAN COINAGE.

[*•* The following slight sketch of the history and coinage of Parthia is put together mainly from three sources: first, the personal researches of the writer among the coins of the British Museum, the Bibliothèque Nationale, etc.; second, the catalogue by the late Count von Prokesch Osten of his own collection; third, Professor Rawlinson's recent history of Parthia. The writer regrets that he has been unable to visit the Museums of Germany and Russia, which doubtless contain many coins unknown to him. He has been obliged to make much use of Count Osten's book, on account of the number of rare and unpublished coins in it, of many of which casts have been kindly forwarded by Dr. Friedländer; but the book is full of small errors and misprints, which have been a continual stumbling-block. Prof. Rawlinson's history has been most valuable, especially because of the copiousness of his references, although he has fallen into a certain number of numismatic errors. The collection of Parthian coins in the British Museum was arranged by the late Count de Salis in accordance with the opinions of M. de Longpérier; and no doubt, if the truth were known, much of what is best in the following pages would be found to be due to the latter savant's ingenuity and experience.]

I. THE AUTHORITIES FOR PARTHIAN HISTORY.

THERE is scarcely any branch of history to which more aptly than to the Parthian can be applied the old saying that history consists of recognized fictions. The course of Parthian annals may be compared to that of a narrow stream passing through a succession of lakes, but itself almost dried up by the summer heat. Where the history of Parthia touches, as it so often does, the annals of Syria and Rome, it suddenly becomes clear and satisfactory. But these reservoirs of knowledge are connected by a thin stream of narrative which often ceases altogether, so that sometimes we are left for a quarter of a century to a chance reference of Lucian, an obscure passage of Josephus, or the sometimes ambiguous evidence of coins. The only consecutive history of the earlier Arsacid kings is the meagre narrative of Justinus, who frequently contradicts both himself and the author, Trogus Pompeius, whom he professes to abridge. Of the later Arsacid kings there is no consecutive history in existence; we have to piece together as best we may scattered notices of Tacitus, Dio, and Josephus.

Nor is anything to be gained by consulting Oriental writers. Moses of Choren cannot indeed be quite neglected, for he occasionally gives us a useful hint; but his value as an authority may be judged from the one fact that he discusses at length the question whether

Crœsus was conquered by Cyrus or by Artaxias, father of the Great Tigranes of Armenia, and finally inclines to the latter opinion. Arabic and Persian writers, so far as one who can consult them only in translations may judge, are wilder still. They probably had no means of ascertaining the truth as to the events of the Parthian period. But had they known the truth, they would have distorted it. They were ashamed to own that Asia was so long under Scythic rule; and so not only very much abridge the duration of the Parthian Empire, and reduce the number of its rulers, but they even venture to furnish us with wholly fanciful lists of kings, in which pure Persian names, such as Firuz and Hormazd, figure largely.

And to conclude, there are scarcely, except coins, any certain historical monuments of Parthian times. Setting aside the rock sculpture of Gotarzes and the ruins of Hatra, there is scarcely a stone or brick in Asia which bears witness to Parthian handiwork. Inscriptions there are next to none. Even in the case of the coins, their value as historical evidence is very much diminished by the fact that hardly any, until the close of the first century of our era, bear any name but the generic name of Arsaces. But the coins almost invariably give portraits, and, after the reign of Orodes, the tetradrachms bear dates, so that their testimony is after all of great value. And as far as it goes it is beyond dispute. The historian is bound to prefer the testimony of a single undoubtedly genuine coin to the statements of a Tacitus or a Thucydides; how much rather to the statements of a Justin or a Plutarch. In the present paper I shall therefore push to the utmost every inference which can legitimately be drawn from existing coins, being careful, however, not to be led astray by the ardour of the specialist in his pursuit.

II. OUTLINE OF HISTORY.

The phrases "History of Parthia," "Coinage of Parthia," are apt to convey a false impression to the unwary ear. Properly speaking, Parthia was a strip of country some hundreds of miles east of the southern extremity of the Caspian Sea, inhabited by a hardy and enterprizing race of Scythic origin. Of the history of this district we know little; nor can we be sure that any coins were ever struck there in ancient times. But for five centuries the race of the Arsacidæ, perhaps of Parthian blood, and certainly owing their sway to Parthian armies, occupied that position of supremacy or over-lordship in Central Asia which has fallen in turn to so many peoples—Tartar, Semitic and Arian. For five centuries the Parthian guard was the most highly esteemed portion of the Asiatic armies; Parthian satraps and garrisons held in subjection the provinces which lie between Syria and India; while all the cities within that region paid tribute to the Arsacid King of Kings, and struck money bearing his name and type. For five centuries a people, or rather a camp, without past or future, without a religion, an art, or a policy of its own, assumed the protectorate of the East, and saved Asia from the arms of Rome. But this people did not colonize, did not attempt to impose a language or a polity on the vanquished, left no trace on Asiatic thought. The so-called History of Parthia is thus really the history of Central Asia under the dominion of the Arsacidæ. The so-called Coinage of Parthia consists of the coins struck under the control of the Arsacid Kings in the cities and camps of Asia. Neither have anything to do with Parthia proper before the revolt of Arsaces or after the revolt of Artaxerxes.

As to the race of the Parthians, the balance of evidence is in favour of their Scythic origin. Justin, Strabo, and Arrian all affirm it. The Parthians themselves believed that they were of Scythic stock. Archæological evidence tends to confirm this hypothesis, both negatively and positively. The negative evidence is the almost absolute want of any traces of a national art. Architecture and sculpture cease in the East during the Parthian period, or appear only in feeble imitations of the Greek. It is the especial peculiarity of conquering Scythian and Tartar tribes thus to leave no trace on the higher growth of the subject peoples. And positively, whenever we find on coin or bas-relief a Parthian King, he is dressed in attire which appears to indicate Scythian descent. It is further to be observed that the Arsacid Kings, whenever hard-pressed by their enemies, were sure of a refuge and an auxiliary force if they fled to the barbarian tribes of the far north and east.

Few dates are harder to fix from the testimony of the ancient writers than that of the Parthian revolt. Some refer it to the reign of Antiochus II. of Syria, some to that of Seleucus, his successor. Justin appears to declare for either 256 or 250 B.C., and it is to the latter date that the latest authorities, as Fynes Clinton and Prof. Rawlinson, incline. The question might probably never have received a satisfactory solution, but for a fortunate discovery (one of the latest, alas!) of George Smith.[1] He found a record which proved that the Parthians made use of an era of which the 144th year corresponded to the 208th of the Seleucid era, and which therefore must date from 249-8 B.C. This positive evidence seems to me to override the authority of contending historians. Perhaps, however, a doubt may suggest itself whether the commencement of the national era of Parthia would be dated from the revolt of Arsaces, or from that victory of his successor over Seleucus Callinicus, which the Parthian nation[2] "velut initium libertatis observant." Such a doubt would however at once be resolved by our knowledge of the fact that Seleucus did not ascend the throne of Syria until the year B.C. 247, and his Parthian expedition cannot be placed earlier than the following year. It is probable then that 248-9 B.C. was the year, if not of the first revolt of Arsaces, at least of the dawn of success on his endeavour.

Arsaces seems to have been the chief or ruler of a band of Scythians, who dwelt near the Ochus,[3] and were a branch of the tribe of Dahæ. Justin says that he was a robber and of uncertain origin, but this is likely enough to have been a calumny by enemies who could not appreciate the fine distinction between Tartar warfare and robbery. Arrian[4] seems to have ascribed to him a royal Persian lineage, but we need not accept a story which, if not true, would have been certain to have been invented. Arsaces' progress was at first slow, impeded by former rulers and new rivals, and he is said to have fallen in battle after a reign of but two

---

[1] G. Smith, Assyrian Discoveries, 1875, p. 389.   [2] Justin, xli. 4.   [3] Strabo, xi. 9, 2.   [4] Syncellus, Chron. p. 284.

years, leaving his half-formed kingdom to his brother Tiridates.[1] His capital was the Greek
city of Hecatompylus.

Tiridates was the real founder of the Parthian power. His first exploit was the conquest
of Hyrcania, which lies to the west of Parthia proper. But he had soon to undergo that
test of invasion by which the vitality of all new states is tried. Seleucus Callinicus of Syria
prepared in 246 a great eastern expedition against Parthia and Bactria. As always happened
in the Syrian expeditions against Parthia, he was at first successful in the field. He forced
Tiridates to fly to the territory of the Aspiacæ, a Scythian tribe. But he seems to have been
less fortunate in a second encounter, when he suffered a great defeat—a defeat which the
Parthian nation thenceforward considered as its "baptism of blood" and initiation into liberty,
and himself became a prisoner in Parthia. Our testimony for this captivity is not strong,[2]
but it is confirmed by the fact that Polybius terms Callinicus 'Pogon,' the bearded; and there
is in the British Museum a tetradrachm representing him as wearing a long beard, a custom
adopted only by those Kings of Syria who were captives in Parthia. In any case Seleucus
soon returned to spend the rest of his reign in contests with his brother Antiochus Hierax,
and Tiridates was left in security to mould his new kingdom. He built a fresh capital, Dara,[4]
and is said to have reigned for as much as thirty-seven years.[5]

It must, nevertheless, be observed that the name and exploits of this King rest only on the
authority of Syncellus, who, however, seems to be following Arrian. Other writers, Moses of
Choren, Strabo, Justin himself, confuse the first and second Kings of Parthia under the one
name Arsaces, and suppose the revolted founder of the monarchy to have defeated Callinicus
and ruled for many years afterwards. The confusion probably arises from the fact that every
King of Parthia bore, besides his particular name, the general one of Arsaces, just as the Kings
of Egypt bore the name Ptolemæus, and the Emperors of Rome the name Cæsar. Most of
the Parthian Kings are usually spoken of by writers as Arsaces or "the Parthian," and it can
scarcely be wondered that this fact has led to some of them being confused together or
entirely overlooked. It is probable that Tiridates was the first to adopt the designation "Great
King," while the title "King of Kings" was not assumed until after the victories of Mithradates I. Both these titles have a historic meaning. They show that the Arsacidæ claimed
to succeed to that lordship which the successors of Cyrus had enjoyed, and to be the legitimate
inheritors of the traditions of the great Asiatic monarchies. But the terms have also a simple
and descriptive application. The Arsacid was in fact, not in word only, the master of a
number of under-kings or satraps, each of whom was almost supreme in his own territory, and
as compared with these little rulers, he might well be termed Great.

Tiridates was succeeded by his son, whom Justin calls Arsaces only, but who is named in
the epitome of Trogus Pompeius, Artabanus. This monarch was called upon to contend with
an even more dangerous antagonist than Callinicus, Antiochus the Great of Syria, at a time

---

[1] Syncellus, Chron. p. 284. [2] Strabo, xi. 8, 8. [3] Posidonius ap. Athen. Deipn. iv. p. 153A. [4] Justin, xli. 5. [5] Syncellus, 284B.

before he had been humbled by the Roman arms. Polybius gives an account of the campaign,[1] which ended, as usual, after a series of barren victories won by the Greeks, in the substantial advantage of Parthia. We are told[2] that Antiochus made an ally of his enemy; at any rate a considerable period elapsed before a Syrian monarch again molested the Eastern Power.

The fourth King of Parthia was Phraapates or Priapatius. Of him we are told nothing except that he reigned fifteen years, and left two sons, who in turn succeeded him. Of these, Phraates I., the elder, conquered the Mardi, and removed them, after the manner of Oriental despots, to Charax.[3] The Parthian succession was not strictly one of primogeniture. The new King must be an Arsacid; but if the sons of the deceased monarch were young or unpopular, a brother or a cousin was often substituted by the aristocratic council. So Phraates was succeeded, even it is said at his own request, by his brother Mithradates I.

The reign of Mithradates witnessed the expansion of the Parthian dominions into a mighty empire. His first war was with the Medes, who, being vanquished, were obliged to accept a king of his choosing, one Bacasis, and probably lost most of the privileges of independence. The Elymæi, the people of Susiana, who apparently had established themselves in independence of the Kings of Syria, were next reduced. Far to the east, Eucratides, the able King of Bactria, was compelled by force of arms to cede Turiua and Aspionus, districts of Bactria.[4] Diodorus[5] even states that Mithradates advanced into the region of India where Porus had ruled. He reigned supreme, as Justin says, from the Himalayas to the Euphrates.

Mithradates set the fashion, which almost all his Parthian successors followed, whenever they were particularly prosperous, of overrunning Armenia. It became one of the fixed ideas of Parthian politics that the King of Armenia should be, if possible, a near relation of the ruling Arsacid; at all events devoted to his service, and resolute in protecting him against aggression by the peoples of the West. Mithradates placed on the throne of Armenia his brother Valarsaces, whom Moses,[6] with a perhaps pardonable patriotic exaggeration, makes ruler of an empire which stretched from the Caspian to the Mediterranean. It is to be observed, however, that the name of this prince is mentioned by no other writer, and that whatever rests upon the unsupported assertion of the Armenian historian has small claim on our belief.

Mithradates was equally fortunate in his dealings with Syria. The Syrian throne was at this time occupied by the young Demetrius Nicator, who was anxious to stop, by a striking example, the secession of small states from the yoke of the Seleucid family. He defeated the great Parthian king in many battles,[7] but at length was captured, through treachery, and detained in a captivity, which was made light to him in order that he should retain a not unkindly feeling for the Parthian king in case the latter should find it desirable to bring him back to his kingdom. He even received in marriage the Parthian princess Rhodogune. The expedition of Demetrius is assigned to the year B.C. 140, and Mithradates did not long survive

---

[1] Polybius, x. 27, 28.   [2] Justin, xli. 5.   [3] Isid. Char. Mans. Parth. 7.   [4] Strabo, xi. 11, 2.
[5] Diodor. xxxiii. 20.   [6] Moses of Choren, ii. 3-7, French translation.   [7] Justin, xxxvi. 1.

his crowning success. He died in a glorious old age, and left a name second only to that of his ancestor, the first Arsaces. It is stated in the Epitome of Trogus Pompeius that 'Tigranes,' King of Parthia, assumed the epithet 'deus.' This word Tigranes would seem to have crept in by mistake in the place of Mithradates. We have numismatic reasons for supposing that Mithradates did in fact claim divinity, in that merely following the example set by such monarchs as Antiochus Theos of Syria.

Phraates II., son of the last monarch, succeeded him, and inherited not only his dominions, but his wars, and the captive Demetrius; whose brother, Antiochus Sidetes, shortly set out for Parthia with a large army, less probably in order to rescue his brother, than to get into his power a rival who might at any time be pitted against him. Like his brother, Antiochus began with a series of victories. It is a most astonishing fact that the Parthians, who so often contended on equal terms with Rome, seem to have been unable to look an army of Syrian Greeks in the face. But his troops, dispersing into winter-quarters in the heart of Asia, were cut to pieces in detail, and himself lost his life in a gallant contest. Among his women who were captured by the Parthian king was a daughter of Demetrius, by whose beauty Phraates was at once captivated, and whom he made his Queen. Meanwhile Demetrius himself had been sent into Syria to raise a faction against his absent brother, and though Phraates afterwards repented of letting his captive go, the repentance came too late.

Not that there was now much to fear from any Syrian king. The flower of the army of the Seleucidæ had fallen or been captured under Sidetes, and the Syrian empire was fast falling to pieces. Parthia was never again invaded by Greeks. But a more terrible foe was approaching from the East. In the second century[1] B.C. the Huns began that westward migration which precipitated them many centuries later on the decaying Roman Empire. Near the borders of China they pressed on the Sakas, the Scythian tribes of Turkestan, and drove them southward upon the Parthian and Bactrian Empires. The latter they completely subverted, and we know from coins that at the beginning of the Christian era Sakas were ruling all Bactria and Northern India.[2] Parthia narrowly escaped the same fate. A band of Saka mercenaries was summoned by Phraates to aid him against the Syrian arms. Arriving too late to be of service to the Parthian king, they quarrelled with him, and he was compelled to march against them, dragging with him the captive remnant of Antiochus' army. These Greeks, as might have been expected, took the opportunity of the first battle to go over to the enemy, and Phráates fell by their hands, leaving the kingdom to his uncle, Artabanus II.

This old warrior does not seem to have been molested by either the Greeks or the Scythians, who were the enemies of the late king. The enmity of both Scythians and Greeks was probably directed personally against Phraates and satisfied by his death. Artabanus, however, soon found himself embarked on a war with another barbarous tribe, the Thogarii, who are mentioned by Strabo[3] as being one of the four great Saka tribes. After a brief reign, he fell

---

[1] Wilson, Ariana Antiqua, p. 141.   [2] Numismatic Chronicle, 1874, pp. 161–167.   [3] Strabo, xi. 8, 2.

in battle against these barbarians. It would seem that during all the reign of Artabanus a sort of imperium in imperio had been going on. Phraates, when he set out against the Scythians, had left as viceroy (vicarius) at Babylon a young Hyrcanian named Himerus. In the troubles which followed, this viceroy appears to have enjoyed a practical independence. He made war on his own account on Mesene,[1] and perpetrated all kinds of cruelties against the people of Babylon and Seleucia, even going so far as to sell whole families into slavery. He is spoken of by some writers as a Parthian king,[2] and there is reason to believe that in the year in which Artabanus fell, B.C. 123, he issued money bearing his own effigy, with the dynastic title of Arsaces.

The Parthian state was now in great peril, and might have fallen to pieces, but for the talents of the great Mithradates II., who succeeded his father Artabanus. His first task was to drive back the Sakas, whom he defeated in many battles, and from whom he wrested no inconsiderable part of Bactria.[3] We know from coins that at about this period several Parthian princes, whose names, Pacores, Gondophares and others, are still to be read, ruled near the Himalayas. Having thus secured his eastern borders, Mithradates turned his attention to Armenia. This country was at that time ruled by a prince called by Justin Artavasdes, but apparently, by native historians, Artaxias, who in any case was probably the descendant and representative of that Artaxias who had successfully revolted against Antiochus III. of Syria. Of the circumstances under which Mithradates attacked him, and of the events of the war, we know nothing beyond the single fact that Artavasdes' son, Tigranes, was a hostage in Parthia,[4] and that hostages are more often given by the defeated than by the victorious State. This same Tigranes, however, when he came to the throne of Armenia, soon turned the tables. He humbled the Parthian power, says Plutarch,[5] more than any enemy before or since, and deprived it of a large part of Asia. Media Atropatane, Susiana, and Mesopotamia, while still remaining under their native princes, paid homage to Tigranes instead of Mithradates.[6] In his dealings with the Kings of Syria, Mithradates was more fortunate. It was to him that Antiochus Eusebes fled after he had lost his throne,[7] and one of his generals carried into captivity Demetrius III.[8]

On the whole, the later years of Mithradates were less prosperous than his earlier ones. Plutarch talks of border and civil wars which wasted the Parthian resources.[9] The epitome of Trogus Pompeius hints at disputed successions and pretenders to the throne. All that we can be certain of is that Mithradates was still King of Parthia in the year 87, to which we can fix, by means of Syrian coins, the captivity of Demetrius. And we have, as will be presently seen, some reason for placing the accession of Sinatroces in the year B.C. 76. We thus get a space of eleven years, which may or may not include the reigns of other kings,

---

[1] Trogus Pompeius, prolog. [2] Posidonius, frag. 21. Diodorus, xxxiv. 21. [3] Strabo, xi. 9, 2.
[4] Strabo, xi. 14, 15. Justin, xxxviii. 3, 1. [5] Plutarch, Lucull. 14 and 21. [6] Strabo, l. c.
[7] Porphyrius Tyrius in Eusebius. [8] Josephus, Ant. Jud. 13, 14. [9] Plutarch, Lucull. 36.

whose names have not come down to us. But it is a most unwarrantable proceeding to insert at this point, as most historians of Parthia do, the name of Mnaskires. The late writer Lucian,[1] when making a list of persons who have lived to a great age, mentions one Mnaskires, or, according to a better reading, Kamnaskires, King of the Parthians, who died at the age of ninety-six. And Prof. Rawlinson observes that there is no room for the insertion of a king at any point of Parthian history except the present. This vague sort of argument however conveys little force to my mind. Moreover, we are acquainted from coins with a Kamnaskires who was, if not a king of Parthia, probably a ruler of a part of the Parthian Empire. These coins are discussed lower down; here I can only say that I regard two things as certain, first, that Kamnaskires was a contemporary of Antiochus III.-V. of Syria, and secondly, that he was not one of the Arsacidæ, but ruler of a tract on the borders of Syria. It is to be observed that Lucian mentions him not among the Kings of Parthia, for whom another paragraph is reserved, but among the Kings of Characene. I have no doubt that the term Παρθναίων is loosely used to indicate some people beyond the eastern boundary of Syria; every classical scholar knows how loosely the term Parthus was used by the Latin writers of the Augustan epoch. Mnaskires is therefore wholly to be removed from the list of the Arsacidæ; nor have we the smallest reason for supposing that Mithradates II. ceased to reign until Sinatroces was called to the throne. This view is well supported by the coins.

It may reasonably be concluded, from a valuable passage of Phlegon,[2] combined with one of Lucian,[3] that Sinatroces reigned for seven years from B.C. 76 to 69. He was at the time of Mithradates' death eighty years of age, and apparently a fugitive or hostage among the Scythian tribe of the Sacaraucæ (Sacarauli?). Perhaps younger Arsacidæ were not to be found, but clearly Sinatroces was not without a rival, for he owed his elevation to the support of his barbarian friends. Of his reign we know absolutely nothing.

He was succeeded by his son Phraates III. As we have now reached the stirring period of the Mithradatic wars of Pompeius, we begin to hear more of Parthia and her king. He had scarcely ascended the throne, when young Tigranes, son of the great Armenian king, claimed his protection and succour against his father.[4] Phraates was easily persuaded to invade Armenia, and penetrated as far as Artaxata. Failing to take that city, he retired into his own territory, and young Tigranes, a second time fugitive, sought the Roman camp.[5] Pompeius was at this period at the height of his power, and seems to have settled the boundaries of the various states of Asia according to his own caprice. Between the elder Tigranes and Phraates, who were once more at open war, he did not choose to interfere; but he resolved that neither should have the province of Gordyene, which he handed over to the King of Cappadocia.[6] We know that Phraates did not live much later than this time, but are

---

[1] Lucian, Macrob. 16: καὶ Μνασκίρης δὲ βασιλεὺς Παρθναίων ἓξ καὶ ἐνενήκοντα ἔζησεν ἔτη. An almost certain correction, suggested by Mr. Vaux in the Num. Chron., is Καμνασκίρης δὲ, etc.   [2] Phlegon fragm. apud Photium cod. 97.

[3] Lucian, Macrob. 15.   [4] Appian, Bell. Mithr. 104.   [5] Dio Cass. xxxvi. 34–5.   [6] Appian, Bell. Mithr. 105–6.

ignorant what was the final issue of his wars with Tigranes. It is possible that the great successes of Tigranes against the Parthians above mentioned may have taken place at this time; but far more likely that Phraates used the opportunity of recovering the provinces which Tigranes had wrested from him before Armenia had been so severely handled by Pompeius. Phlegon tells us that Phraates III. assumed the title θεός.

Phraates was murdered by his sons, Mithradates and Orodes. According to Dio,[1] Orodes succeeded him; but we are justified in preferring the account of Justin, Appian and Plutarch, that his immediate successor was Mithradates. The latter, however, would seem to have soon disgusted, by his cruelty, the Parthian nobility, whose hereditary chief, the Surena or Grand Marshal, recalled[2] Orodes from exile, and succeeded in placing him on the throne. For a time Mithradates managed to maintain himself in Media; but the arms of Orodes soon expelled him hence[3] also. He fled to Gabinius, who then governed Syria, and tried to persuade him to reinstate him; but Gabinius found more tempting opportunities in another direction, and declined to stir.[4] Justin says that Orodes besieged his brother in Babylon, took him prisoner, and put him to death. Whether this took place after the negociations with Gabinius, or whether it is another and independent account of the circumstances under which Orodes entered into his kingdom, it is now impossible to determine. In any case the most illustrious reign in the Parthian annals opens in a sinister manner enough.

The accession of Orodes may be placed about the year B.C. 55. He had scarcely had time to consolidate his power and reduce the great cities, which, like Babylon and Seleucia, held out for his brother, when the great Roman army of Crassus invaded the Parthian dominions from the west. Orodes divided his forces. Himself marched into Armenia, coming to terms with the King of that country after a little fighting, while the Surena advanced at the head of the Parthian mounted archers to encounter Crassus. The fate of the Roman legions is well known, and it at first seemed probable that Crassus' death would be followed by the total expulsion of the Romans from Asia. While Europe was convulsed by the rivalries of Pompeius and Cæsar, and Rome was squandering the blood of her best legions in civil wars, Asia was left almost defenceless, and the Parthian armies, under Pacorus, the son and future colleague[5] of Orodes, carried all before them. Cicero, at that time proconsul of Cilicia, gives us in his letters[6] a vivid picture of the terror spread by the barbarian army. But after wintering in Cyrrhestica the young Parthian prince was recalled (B.C. 50) by the jealousy of his father, and the Romans enjoyed for nine years a peace which must have been most grateful to them.

In a second and more persistent invasion, which was headed by Pacorus and Labienus, an old general of Cæsar, the Parthians penetrated still further to the west. Syria was subdued, Asia Minor was overrun, the government of Judæa was overturned, and Antigonus set up in

---

[1] Dio C. xxxix. 56.   [2] Plutarch Cras. 21.   [3] Dio C. xxxix. 56.   [4] Appian, Syr. 51.

[5] Pacorus is termed *rex* by Tacitus (Hist. v. 9), and that Tacitus is right is proved by the legend of Orodes' coins, and the pieces with Pacorus' effigy. We do not know *when* he was associated in the government.

[6] Ad diversos xv. 1–4, ad Att. v. 21.

GARDNER   2

the high priesthood,[1] and the Romans encountered nothing but disaster, until the arrival of Ventidius. Then, however, fortune at once changed sides. Labienus, who had gone so far as to strike in Syria gold coins bearing his own portrait, as if he supposed himself the equal of the rulers of Rome, was first slain, and soon after Pacorus fell in the midst of a gallant attack. Having lost their leaders, the Parthian troops hastily retreated homewards. Nor was Orodes less crushed than his army by the loss of Pacorus. None of his other sons seemed worthy to mount the throne, and he knew not which to prefer. When, at length, he had selected Phraates, that prince, fearing perhaps lest his father's mind should change, had him assassinated in the year B.C. 37. The coins of Orodes give one the impression, which is otherwise confirmed, that he was a great administrator, the second κτιστής of the Parthian power after the first Mithradates, and that in his time the Parthian rule took a new vitality, which sustained it for centuries in rivalry to the great power of Rome, which acknowledged no other equal.

Phraates IV. began his reign in true Oriental fashion, by murdering all his brothers, as a necessary precaution before he began murdering other people. The invasion of Antonius occurred in the first year of his reign. It ended not so disastrously, indeed, as had that of Crassus, but yet in a manner little likely to raise his military reputation. His retreat is said so to have inflamed the vanity and ferocity of the Parthian King, that the latter became intolerable to his people, who set up in his absence one Tiridates, who was probably an Arsacid,[2] and who seems to have issued tetradrachms in the year 32 B.C. Not long after, Phraates returned with a Scythian army, and Tiridates took refuge with Augustus. It is worthy of note that a genuine Arsacid seems at all times to have been able to collect an army among the Sakas of the east. Later, when Augustus had put down all his rivals, and was beginning to consider the advisability of a fresh invasion of Parthia, Phraates thought it prudent to adopt every means of conciliation. He restored the prisoners and the standards of Crassus, and sent as hostages to Rome four of his sons,[3] among whom was Vonones, with their wives and children.

He married late in life an Italian slave, called by Josephus, Thermusa,[4] but whose name is given as Thea Musa on coins. The latter may well have been an adopted name, just as some of the Kings of Syria adopted the name of Apollo or Dionysus.[5] Whatever her name, she must have had talent; and her effigy and name are the sole memorial left to us of the Queens of Parthia. Her son Phraataces was made heir, to the detriment of the elder sons of the King, and proceeded on this to assassinate his father.

With Phraates the dates on Parthian tetradrachms become usual, and are of the greatest value for determining the length of the reigns of kings and other points in chronology. No

---

[1] Josephus, B. J. i. 13, 1.   [2] Justin xlii. 5.
[3] Strabo, xvi. 1, 28. The names of two of these sons, Seraspadanes and Rhodaspes, occur in an inscription now at Rome.
[4] Josephus, A. J. xviii. 2, 4. I believe that the MS. reading is ΘΕΣΜΟΥΣΑ; and there is great probability in the suggestion of M. de Longpérier that this may be a mere corruption of ΘΕΑ ΜΟΥΣΑ. The name Thermusa does not sound Italian.
[5] Mr. Thomas gives another explanation in his Early Sassanian Inscriptions, p. 122, and prefers ΘΕΑC ΜΟΥCΗC.

better proof of this can be given than is afforded by the old opinions as to the dates of Phraataces, Orodes II., and Vonones. Mr. Fynes Clinton, summing up the testimony of writers with his usual ability, assigned all these to the period A.D. 15–17. We know, from dated coins, that Phraataces was king as early as August B.C. 2, and that Vonones was set up as early as 8/9 A.D.

Phraataces at first ruled under the direction of his Latin mother, and in fact throughout his reign her effigy appears with his on the coins—a thing quite new to Parthia, where habits of polygamy made women of small account. Hence, probably, he was from the first unpopular, and continually in fear of the return of some of his brothers from Rome. When Caius, the grandson of Augustus, was in Syria arranging the affairs of the East, Phraataces eagerly took the opportunity of coming to terms with him, meeting him on a little island in the midst of the Euphrates.[1] He was ready to concede almost anything for the sake of peace, and agreed to evacuate Armenia, and that his brothers should remain at Rome.[2] He was killed in an insurrection, apparently A.D. 4, and Orodes, who had been his rival, succeeded him for a few years. At this period the Parthian Empire seems to have been much harassed, not by civil wars alone, but also from the East by Parthian rulers, probably the descendants of those who, about the time of Mithradates II., had settled in Bactria. In the year 1/2 A.D. one of these chiefs named Sanabares struck money closely imitating the true Arsacid coinage—a fact which seems to show that he, too, was a claimant of the crown of Parthia.

Orodes offended his people by intolerable cruelties,[3] and was assassinated, either at a banquet or a hunting excursion, in the year 7/8 A.D. On his death, the Parthian nobility sent an embassy to Rome, requesting Augustus to give them as king one of the sons of Phraates IV. Vonones was sent, and entered on his kingdom at first without opposition. But his Roman education and urbane manners quite unfitted him for ruling a race of Scythic blood, and the nobles soon made up their minds to substitute for him an Arsacid named Artabanus, who dwelt at a distance, either in Media, as Josephus says, or, according to the preferable account of Tacitus,[4] among the Dahæ, a Saka tribe of the far east. That Artabanus was at first defeated we know both from the statement of Tacitus, and from the inscription on the coins which Vonones struck to commemorate his victory, νεικήσας Ἀρταβάνου. The date of these coins ranges from 9 to 11 A.D. Before the end of the latter year, however, Artabanus made a second attempt, with the assistance of a Scythian army, and Vonones considered flight to be his wisest policy. Stopping first at Seleucia, and afterwards having been even acknowledged as King in a district of Armenia, he was at last obliged to avoid the incessant pursuit of his rival by taking refuge in Syria.

Artabanus III., whose first coins are dated 10/11 A.D., was a vigorous ruler, and of more strongly defined personality than most of the Parthian kings. We find him negociating with Germanicus shortly before the death of the latter.[5] After this he engaged in wars of a suc-

---

[1] Vel. Paterc. ii. 101.   [2] Dio C. lv. 11, Sturz's edition. Earlier editions have Phraates' name in the place of Phraataces'.
[3] Josephus, A. J. xviii. 2, 4.   [4] Tacitus, Ann. ii. 3.   [5] Tac. Ann. ii. 58.

cessful issue with several of the neighbouring states, and made an attack upon Armenia, whence he was, however, expelled by Pharasmanes.[1] These signs of aggressiveness induced Tiberius to listen to the Parthian malcontents, who were constantly clamouring that another of the sons of Phraates IV. should be introduced by Roman arms. Phraates was first selected, but he died of disease in Syria. Next Tiridates, a grandson of Phraates IV., was introduced into Parthia by Vitellius, the Governor of Syria. Artabanus fled without striking a blow, but the absence of any coins apparently struck by Tiridates makes it most probable that his rule was either very short or very incomplete. It is probable that in this, as in other cases,[2] Tacitus has somewhat exaggerated the success of the Roman arms. Artabanus was soon recalled by the nobles, and Tiridates took refuge in Syria. Indeed, at one time a Parthian invasion of Syria was feared, but was averted by the promptness and decision of Vitellius, who even extorted from Artabanus a profession of homage to the Roman Emperor. Once more, for a short period, Artabanus was a fugitive, a certain noble named Cinnamus[3] being elected in his place; but the latter prevented a civil war by a voluntary abdication, himself placing the diadem on his master's head. At the same date, A.D. 40, the great city of Seleucia, on the Tigris, revolted against the Parthian rule, and retained an autonomy, of which we possess numismatic records, for the space of six years.

Artabanus must have died as early as A.D. 40, for we have coins of his successor under that date. Who that successor was has been disputed. It is certain that a civil war took place between Vardanes and Goterzes, sons of the late king,[4] but it has not been considered certain who reigned first. The coins appear to contradict the account of Josephus, who maintains that Vardanes succeeded, and to confirm that of Tacitus, who interpolates a short first reign of Gotarzes after the death of Artabanus, i.e. in the year 40–41 A.D. Tacitus further relates that after a short time, Gotarzes, having been unpopular in Parthia, was compelled to fly to the friends of his father, the Dahæ. Returning with an army of those barbarians, he met Vardanes in the field, but a battle was avoided by a treaty in which all the concessions seem to have been on one side. Parthia was left to Vonones, and Goterzes, to avoid all rivalry, retired into the wilds of Hyrcania. He seems, however, shortly to have grown tired of inaction, or repented of his magnanimity. Vardanes had marched westward, taken Seleucia, threatened Armenia, and attacked Izates, the powerful Satrap of Gordyene and Atropatene; and Goterzes took advantage of his absence to make a new effort to gain the Parthian throne. This time he was completely successful, Vardanes was assassinated while intent on hunting, apparently in the year 45, and no further resistance was made by his party. But Goterzes used his success ill; and his tyranny produced a new rival in the person of Meherdates, another descendant of Phraates, who was patronized by the Emperor Claudius, and actively supported by Izates. But Meherdates[5] had not penetrated far into Parthia when he was

---

[1] Tac. Ann. vi. 31.   [2] Josephus, A. J. xx. 3, 1.

[3] As in the case of the Roman occupations of Armenia. See Num. Chron. n.s. vol. xii. p. 9 sqq.

[4] Tacitus seems to say of Goterzes 'brother,' Josephus 'son' (cf. Tacitus, Ann. xi. 8, and Josephus, A. J. xx. 3, 4). The coins decide the point.   [5] Tac. Ann. xii. 13.

met and defeated in a pitched battle by Goterzes. He was captured, but saved his life by the sacrifice of his ears, it being impossible that a mutilated person should ever bear rule over Parthians. A record of the victory of Goterzes remains to this day in the rude rock-sculpture which he caused to be executed in honour of the event. This sculpture is cut on some rocks at Behistun right upon figures which date from the reign of Darius Hystaspes, and obliterating them. It consists of a king on horseback, with lance couched, galloping in pursuit of a wild animal, while Victory hovers above him and places a wreath on his head. Behind him gallops a smaller horseman.[1] Above is a much mutilated inscription, which is still further destroyed by having an arch or doorway cut through the middle of it. Sir Henry Rawlinson, who visited the spot thirty years ago, read the inscription thus:[2] ΑΛΦΑΣΑΤΗΣ ΜΙΘΡΑΤΗΣ ΠΕΠ . . . . ΓΩΤΑΡΖΗC ΣΑΤΡΑΠΗΣ ΤΩΝ ΣΑΤΡΑΠ and further found below the words ΓΩΤΑΡΣΗC ΓΕΟΠΟΘΡΟΣ. This latter word the writer supposes to represent the Persian Gívputr (son of Gív); Gúdarz ibn Gív being renowned in Persian fable. But it will be seen from the very careful drawing of M. Flandin that not all the letters seen by Rawlinson are now visible. So far as I am aware, no one has yet succeeded in translating this inscription; the editors of it content themselves with pointing out the name of Meherdates in its debased form ΜΙΘΡΑΤΗΣ, and commenting on the assumption by Goterzes of the title Satrap of Satraps—a title which is but another indication of the decay of letters at this period in Asia.

Soon after this, Gotarzes died, and was succeeded by Vonones II., a prince probably of Arsacid blood, and at the time of his elevation Satrap of Media. His reign, says Tacitus, was short and inglorious. It terminated in the year 51; for we know, both from the assertions of Tacitus[3] and from extant coins, that in this year his son, Vologeses, was already on the throne. This Vologeses seems to have been preferred to his brothers in virtue of a family pact, by which it was arranged that Pacorus should have Media, Vologeses Parthia, and that for Tiridates Armenia should be acquired by force of arms. The carrying out of the last article of the agreement caused a war of many years against Rome, in which fortune bestowed her favours in turn on the combatants. But the solid advantage rested with Parthia, for Tiridates was acknowledged by Nero as King of Armenia in return for a personal homage,[4] which, though couched in servile terms, probably hampered him very little in his practical politics. Many other wars occupied this most bellicose of reigns. Vologeses had a long contest with Izates, who had become too powerful for a mere subject, and who died unsubdued. He also had to withstand an invasion of the Scythian Dahæ, who, after overrunning Armenia, were scarcely to be kept from devastating Parthia. These difficulties were further complicated by the revolt of his own son, Vardanes, whose independence, as we may judge from his coins, stood firm during the years 55–58, but afterwards fell. Several other events must be assigned to this important reign. In the year 70, when Vespasian was setting out to seek the purple,

---

[1] Figured in the frontispiece. This figure is copied from the noble work of Flandin and Coste (Perse Ancienne), plate xix.
[2] Journal of the Geographical Society, vol. ix. p. 114. [3] Tac. Ann. xii. 44, 50. [4] Dio C. lxiii. 6.

ambassadors reached him from Vologeses, offering him an aid of 40,000 Parthian horse, an offer which Vespasian had the good sense to decline.[1] And as he on this occasion declined aid, he was able in turn to refuse to give it some time later, when Vologeses, hard pressed by the Alani, who had overrun Media, begged the loan of some Roman soldiery,[2] with Titus or Domitian as captain. It must have been at about the same time that Hyrcania threw off the Parthian yoke, for Josephus,[3] writing of the fourth year of Vespasian's reign, speaks of an independent King of the Hyrcanians, who may very probably have been a new barbarian invader. It was also the first Vologeses who built the city of Vologesocerta.[4]

A curious question has vexed the Parthian historians, namely, whether this Vologeses I. reigned until Pacorus mounted the throne, about 77 A.D., or whether other kings occupied part of that period. We know from the statements of Tacitus that *a* Vologeses was king after 70, but some numismatists have supposed that there are in the coins such differences in type and the portrait of the king, before the year 60 and after it, that we must suppose a second and younger Vologeses to have succeeded the first at that time. Others, most unreasonably, have termed this second king Artabanus. But to procure the insertion of a king not known to historians numismatic evidence should be strong and undeniable; and it may be doubted if such is here the case. I shall resume this subject hereafter, in the strictly numismatic part of the present essay.

We know, on numismatic evidence, that the reign of Pacorus II. extended from May, 78, to February, 96; also, that he was quite a youth at the time of his accession; but regarding the events of his reign, we have little information. He appears to have sold[5] Osrhoene to Abgarus for a large sum of money, which looks as if he were in great straits, and, in fact, Dio tells us[6] that at the time of Trajan's invasion, Parthia had suffered much, and was still suffering from civil wars. This circumstance may explain how it was that, when, in the year 89, a Pseudo-Nero appeared on the Euphrates, and the Parthians were quite inclined to support his claims to the Roman purple, the Parthian King mentioned in this connexion, nameless in Suetonius,[7] is by the late writer, Zonaras,[8] called Artabanus. And however little we might be inclined to accept the mere statement of Zonaras, it is rendered credible by coins which give us the name of Artabanus as Parthian King in 80/81 A.D. Other coins, which seem to belong to this period, or to the early part of the reign of Chosroes, are some drachms bearing in Pehlvi letters the name of a King Mithradates. A copper coin published below, bearing the same head as these drachms, seems to be dated A.S. 424. Of the prince who issued these pieces we have no trustworthy information at all. The name does, indeed, occur in a passage of Malala.[9] This late writer tells us, that in the time of Trajan there was a King of Persia (a Parthian by race) named Meerdotes, who had a son named Sinatruces. Meerdotes fell in battle; Sinatruces captured Antioch from the Romans. Parthamaspates, son of Osdroes, King

---

[1] Tac. Hist. iv. 51.
[4] Pliny, N. H. vi. 26, 122. Pliny speaks of the city as recently built (nuper).
[5] Suidas ad. voc. ἀνητή.
[8] Zonaras, Ann. xi. 18.
[2] Sueton. Domit. 2.
[6] Dio C. lxviii. 26.
[9] Joh. Malala, Chronogr. L. xi.
[3] Josephus, B. J. vii. 7, 4.
[7] Suetonius Nero, 57.

of Armenia, came to the aid of Sinatruces, but quarrelling with him, went over to the Roman side. Malala gives as his authorities, one Domninus, as far as the quarrel of Sinatruces and Parthamaspates, and after that Ἀρειανὸς ὁ χρονογράφος, whom one would naturally suppose to be the historian Arrian. But I do not think that we can attach any value to the confused story of Malala, which is in itself improbable, and is rendered less acceptable by two further considerations. Firstly, it is absurd to suppose that if a Parthian chief had captured Antioch, so important an event would have been passed over in silence by the Roman historians. And secondly, the whole story is distinctly inconsistent with the account of Parthamaspates given in an extant fragment of Arrian. There may have been a germ of truth in Malala's narrative, but it is quite impossible to separate the corn of wheat from the husk. It is curious that in a fragment of Dio (75, 9), it is recorded that Severus fought Vologeses, son of Sinatruces, and afterwards gave him part of Armenia (ἐπὶ τῇ εἰρήνῃ ἐχαρίσατο). If for Severus, we read Verus, we may suppose that Vologeses IV., whose ancestry is unknown, was the son of the Sinatruces mentioned by Malala.

Chosroes, son of Pacorus, succeeded his father as early as 107, and spent a most stormy reign in constant fighting against the relentless and ambitious Emperor Trajan. The subject of dispute was, as usual, Armenia. Chosroes, early in his reign, expelled Exedares, King of that country, explaining, with quiet cynicism, that he was useful neither to Parthia nor to Rome, and proceeded to demand the throne for his brother Parthamasiris. Trajan, having finally reduced Dacia, seized the opportunity of marching a great army into Armenia and Parthia, with the thinly disguised intention of adding Central Asia to the already unwieldy mass of the Roman Empire. It is well known how successful was his advance, how disastrous his retreat. The puppet-prince, Parthamaspates, whom he had set up in Parthia, could not survive his departure, and all that Trajan gained by his expedition was Armenia and most of Mesopotamia,[1] which were held as Roman provinces. Hadrian, however, on his accession, withdrew the Roman legions at once to the Euphrates, exhibiting a rare moderation in the midst of success; part of the territory conquered by his warlike predecessor he restored to Parthia, over part he placed Parthamaspates,[2] who was now a fugitive dependent of Rome. At a later period, Chosroes was inclined to try once more the fortune of war against Rome,[3] but Hadrian, who was then in the East, invited him to a personal conference, and showed him reason for desisting. Hadrian even restored, as a favour, his daughter, who had been carried captive by Trajan—a course of behaviour which produced harmony between Rome and Parthia, and so deprives our history of material for a considerable period.

Coins which bear the portrait of Chosroes continue until the year 127–8. But we have another series partly contemporary with these, and beginning certainly as early as 119–20, which bear quite another portrait, and the name of Vologeses. This latter king, then, must

[1] Dio C. lxviii. 33.
[2] Ael. Spart. Hadrian v. The name of the prince as given in the copies is corrupt, but the context leaves no doubt as to who is meant.
[3] Ael. Spart. Hadrian xii.

have reigned contemporaneously with Chosroes, probably at first in a remote part of the Parthian dominions. After Chosroes' death, he must have reunited all the Empire under his sway, for we find no apparent trace of a rival in the public money. His name is once mentioned by Roman historians. Soon after the year 130, another of those barbarian invasions, which were becoming of alarming frequency in the East, occurred. The Alani descended from the northern wilds, devastating far and wide. We are told that Vologeses bought them off,[1] a sign that he was neither a very powerful nor a very courageous prince. It was probably this Vologeses who demanded the Parthian royal throne, which Trajan had carried off, from Antoninus Pius,[2] and when that great Emperor refused it, began to meditate war.

It would appear from the coins, that in 148 this King was succeeded by a fourth Vologeses, who may have been his son, and who, early in the reign of Marcus Aurelius, having invaded Armenia, and expelled thence the King Soæmus or Syæmus, proceeded to attack the Roman provinces of Syria and Judæa. This led to the eastern expedition of Lucius Verus, and a long war, conducted with unusual skill, by Martius Verus, Cassius, and other Roman generals. The Romans, on this occasion, secured more of the fruits of victory than was their wont, when they opposed Parthia. Soæmus was reinstated by them in Armenia,[3] and the Kings of Edessa became, as we know from numismatic testimony, henceforth the constant vassals of Rome. Vologeses would appear to have been unsatisfied with the course of events, for we learn that ten years later he was again meditating war.[4] But he died with his purpose unaccomplished.

In 190-1 another Vologeses (V.) succeeds. This prince suffered much through allowing himself to be mixed up in the quarrels of the generals who disputed the succession in the Roman Empire after the fall of Commodus. Niger applied to the Kings of Armenia, Hatra, and Parthia for auxiliaries, and the latter promised that they should be sent—a promise which he does not seem to have kept. So Septimius Severus had no sooner disposed of his rivals than he led a new Parthian expedition. Vologeses had been beforehand with him; he had already overrun Mesopotamia, and laid siege to the Roman colony of Nisibis. Severus did not stay in the East very long, or gain a brilliant success; but he sufficiently vindicated the honour of the Roman arms, and retained Adiabene in permanence. It was easy to see that the Parthian power was not what it had been.

On the death of Vologeses in 208-9, the succession was disputed in civil war[5] between his sons, Vologeses VI. and Artabanus IV. Of these, the former seems at first to have been successful, for in the year 215 Caracalla demanded of him the return of some fugitives.[6] But in the following year Artabanus is spoken of by Dio as King of Parthia. It was Artabanus against whom Caracalla fought several pitched battles, when, after seeking a quarrel, and finding one, he engaged in his ambitious eastern expedition. It was the ambition of the life of the Roman madman to imitate Alexander the Great; but his death was more like Alexander's than his life, for he, too, found a Persian grave. Macrinus drew off the Roman army, which

[1] Dio C. lxix. 15. Zonaras, 590c.   [2] Jul. Capit. Antoninus Pius ix.   [3] Suidas ad voc. Μάρτιος.
[4] Jul. Capit. Antoninus Philos. xxii.   [5] Dio C. lxxvii. 12.   [6] Dio C. lxxvii. 19 and 21.

had suffered most severely. But the vitality of Parthia was exhausted with the exertion required to throw off this last of the Roman invasions, and the empire was about to fall. Persia proper had long been a province of the Parthian dominions; but, like Media and other provinces, had been governed by kings of its own, subject only to a tribute and a Parthian garrison. Ardeshir or Artaxerxes raised, about 220 A.D., the banner of revolt against the barbarian conquerors in the name of the ancient lineage and religion of Persia; Artabanus fell in a battle,[1] and the sceptre of the East passed from Parthian into Persian hands in the year 226-7. Not that all resistance on the part of Parthia at once ceased. Doubtless Hyrcania and Parthia proper would hold out long against the new Persian king. We possess a tetradrachm with the date 227-8 and the name of Artavasdes, which must have been struck by a Parthian patriot in a yet unconquered corner of the East; but this is the last monument of Parthia. The nation, when it had once ceased to be victorious, vanished from the field of politics like a dream, leaving, perhaps, fewer lessons and fewer memorials of every kind to posterity than any other dynasty which has reigned, for half a millennium, within historical times.

III. PRELIMINARY OBSERVATIONS ON COINAGE.

It will be best to prefix to a description of the coins issued by the Parthian Kings a brief dissertation. All peculiarities attaching to particular issues will be noted in their place in the detailed description; but a few general remarks are required in this place, on the essential characteristics which run through all the series.

There are no known gold coins of Parthia, and it is at present impossible to say what is the denomination or normal value of the copper pieces. All the silver coins, without exception, follow the Attic standard as adopted by the Kings of Syria, whose tetradrachms weigh about 270, the drachms about 67½, and the obols about 11 grains. Few of the Parthian coins—except in certain reigns the drachms—come near to this standard, and a slight diminution of weight marks the later coins as compared with the earlier. It was not, however, by reducing in Roman method the standard of weight that the Parthians debased their coin. They found it more convenient to allow the metal used to deteriorate in quality. The coins of Tiridates, and even of Mithradates, are of tolerably pure silver; those of the later Kings of a very debased mixture. Together with the debasement of the metal of which the coin is composed, proceeds the deterioration in art and workmanship, which must strike the most superficial observer. The types mostly persist; but they are reproduced by every fresh die-cutter in a more ugly and untruthful form.

The types used by a people on its coin are almost always characteristic, and offer us the most valuable information as to the national customs and beliefs. This is perhaps less the case

---

[1] Herodian vi. 2.

with Parthian types than elsewhere ; nevertheless, we obtain from them some important light on the dress, government, and religion of the country.

All the drachms issued by the Arsacidæ, from first to last, as well as the earlier tetradrachms, bear a uniform type,—Arsaces, the great founder of the empire, seated to right holding in his hand a strung bow. After the reign of Mithradates I., the object on which he is seated is a throne with a back, such as Zeus occupies on the coins of Alexander the Great. But in the earlier drachms it is clearly the omphalos of Apollo, that conical stone at Delphi, which was supposed by the Greeks to be the centre of the world. The introduction of this stone indicates at once whence the Parthians borrowed their type. It is clearly taken from the coins of the Seleucid Kings of Syria, on which Apollo usually appears seated on the omphalos, and holding out a strung bow, just as Arsaces himself does. The Seleucidæ had probably themselves taken the figure from the coins of Nicocles, King of Cyprus, one of which is quoted by Mionnet (vol. iii. last page).

The tetradrachms show more variety, or at least begin to do so at the beginning of the Christian era ; while the copper coins present to us a multitude of types. Without detailing these, I will discuss the light thrown by them on the dress, customs, religion and government of the Parthians.

The costume of the first Arsaces is strongly characteristic. He wears a conical helmet not unlike that of the Assyrians,[1] with flaps to protect ears and neck, and bound with the regal diadema of the Greeks; his ears are adorned with earrings, and his neck with a torquis of the simplest form. He is clad in a coat of mail, apparently consisting of scale or chain armour, which covers his arms to the wrist, and his legs to the ancle ; over this is thrown a short military cloak or sagum. His shoes are fastened by straps or thongs round the ancles. This dress, which suited a rude leader of nomads, rather than an Asiatic King of Kings, was soon abandoned by the successors of Arsaces. Mithradates I. wears on his head either the simple diadema, or a semicircular Parthian helmet, similar to that figured in the frontispiece, studded with many rows of nails, and having leather or iron flaps to protect ears and neck ; also bound with the diadema. On his neck is a spiral torquis, which ends in an ornament shaped like the forepart of a horse. In place of the rude armour he wears a soft under-garment, and an over-garment shaped like a cloak, open at the neck, having sleeves, and adorned apparently with several rows of gems. How the lower part of his body is dressed we cannot tell, as we have no full-length representation of him. Some of his successors wear helmets of a like form, but adorned round the edge with the recumbent figures of stags, or with rows of balls. And some of them, as Mithradates III., wear a jointed torquis, which seems to be made of gems. Mithradates II. appears, like Arsaces, in a full suit of armour.

On the coins of Phraates IV. and his successors we find frequent full-length portraits of Kings, and always in the same costume, which is quite different alike from that of Arsaces

---

[1] Cf. the helmet from the British Museum represented in the frontispiece. That the helmet here represented was Assyrian is proved from the place where it was found, and the remains in which it was imbedded.

and that of Mithradates. The King now wears a soft under-garment, over which is a short jacket or blouse, open at the neck, and there adorned with rows of braid, and tied in at the waist by a girdle. His legs are clad in trousers, full above and tight below, much like those associated in former years with the French soldier. It is curious to compare this regal costume with that of the Parthian subject on the coins of Artabanus III. The chief difference between the two is that the blouse of the subject is much longer, as well as less adorned, reaching far below the hips. The loose trousers are common to master and subject. Chosroes and Vologeses V., among the later Kings, introduced a striking innovation. With the exception of these two, all the Parthian Kings seem to have worn their hair short, or at all events but a few inches long, and hanging in natural waves. But these two princes adopted the fashion of puffing out their hair into huge balls, on either side of the head, or behind it. There can be little doubt that this was a Persian, not a Parthian fashion, for it is very usual on the coins of the Sassanian princes. The name of Chosroes (Cyrus) is also Persian, which makes it the more likely that he should have been, as the ancients would say, Philo-Persian.

The dress of women is less frequently represented on coins. Musa, the wife of Phraates IV., wears a lofty tiara, adorned with gems, and bound with the Syrian diadema; over her shoulders is a rich mantle, open, like her husband's, at the neck. The female figures which occur on the reverse of later tetradrachms, being intended to represent Greek cities, are clad, in Greek fashion, in long chiton and himation. The dress of the true Parthian women may have been different; that of the Queens is, as we have seen.

Such are the data of our coins, and it is interesting to compare them with the statements of ancient writers. Justin says :—"Vestis olim sui moris; posteaquam accessere opes, ut Medis perlucida ac fluida" (xli. 2). This latter dress as not national and as luxurious does not appear on coins, but even the Kings may have used it in private. As the Parthian King was essentially a soldier, and never truly in his place except at the head of his troops, it is fair to suppose that both the coat of mail and sagum of Arsaces I., and the short jacket and loose trousers of the later Kings, were military dress; and this is confirmed by the fact that the monarchs who appear in both dresses sometimes wear a helmet. When the King rides on horseback, he wears the lighter of the two.

Now it is an interesting coincidence with these facts that the Parthian cavalry was divided into two sorts, the heavy and the light. The heavy cavalry (καταφρακτοί) were clad in complete suits of scale or chain armour, and carrying long pikes, bore down the enemy by the weight of their onset. Their charge was like that of the lance-bearing Norman knights, whose prototype indeed they were. The light cavalry wore no armour, and carried no lance; they trusted for victory to their bows. It is very probable that Arsaces is represented in the guise of the heavy, Phraates IV. in that of the light horse; and it would appear that the latter soldiers were found more serviceable and more effective for fighting in the Parthian manner.

The semicircular helmet would seem to have been an invention of Mithradates, or rather an improvement by him upon the conical Assyrian helmet, which is constantly met in the sculptures of Nimroud, and which remained in use probably until Parthian times.

The manners and customs of the Parthians were derived from three distinct sources. They always retained much that derived from their Scythian ancestors; but at the same time they inherited many of the traditions of the Persian and Assyrian races, which had been paramount for centuries in Asia. With these habits mingled others of Greek origin, brought into Asia by the soldiers of Alexander, and maintained there by the cities which he founded. Of all three sets of customs we find traces on the coins. That the King sometimes appears on horseback, and that his favourite weapon is the bow, point clearly to a Scythian source. On the other hand, the scenes in which the monarch, seated, receives gifts and marks of honour from his subjects, are clearly late copies of those reliefs of Assyrian times, of which so many still remain. Of Greek influence the signs are still commoner. The Greek diadema is the type of kingship; the Greek wreath is the reward of valour or merit. All the titles of the monarchs are Greek, and the era by which time is reckoned is the era of the Seleucidæ.

Especially in the indications of Parthian religion do we find a blending of three distinct strains. The Scythian stock has never been noted for fervent attachment to any creed, and seems in early times, from the statements of Herodotus, to have been almost destitute of a creed. What, then, more natural than that those hardy and materialistic warriors, who, under Tiridates and Mithradates, overran Asia, should pay their chief veneration to the highest visible being, the symbol of their wide sovereignty, the King himself, and especially Arsaces, the ancestor of their Kings. Such veneration and worship is clearly implied in the position occupied by Arsaces on the reverse of the Parthian coins, a position exactly similar to that in which the Seleucidæ placed Apollo, whom they regarded as *their* ancestor. Such religion as the Parthians possessed, over and above veneration for their national hero and his family, they adopted from the Persians. Of this we are sure from numerous statements of the historians, but we find extremely few traces of the Persian cult on coins. On the coins, indeed, commonly called sub-Parthian, and issued, in Parthian times, by the Satraps of the Great King, the fire-altar is a usual type. But on the national issues we can point to nothing which indicates fire-worship except perhaps the emblems of sun and moon on the pieces of Orodes, and of some of his successors.

It is more interesting to observe what traces are found on coins of the worship of the Greeks. There are two beings or classes of beings, the creation of Greek imagination, which are especially common on the Parthian coin. The first of these is Nike, who first makes her appearance in the time of Mithradates I., and is afterwards seldom absent for long together. The second is Tyche, the genius of a city, who appears constantly on the pieces of Phraates IV. and his successors, presenting to the reigning King a wreath or the regal diadema. The introduction of these figures, however, can scarcely have a religious meaning; we have no reason for supposing that there were any Parthian temples or priesthoods of Nike or Tyche.

But there are, in a few instances, even on the copper coins which are of the most thoroughly Parthian type, images of some of the great Greek divinities. Pallas, or an armed female deity undistinguishable from Pallas, occurs in the reigns of Phraates IV., Goterzes, and Vologeses II. Artemis makes her appearance under Goterzes. Zeus, or a deity who holds eagle and sceptre, the attributes of the great God, is found on the coins which I give to Vardanes II. A head which might well be that of Apollo, in his character as Sun-God, occurs in the reigns of Phraates IV. and Goterzes. The Roman deities Janus and Æquitas or Nemesis are also portrayed under Phraates. Besides these well-known Greek and Roman types, occur others which would seem to be Greek, but are of a more obscure nature; a male winged genius, who holds a bunch of grapes under Phraates IV. and Artabanus III., and a male figure, probably Harpocrates, who holds cornucopiæ and raises his hand to his head, under Vardanes I. Herakles, Zeus and the Dioscuri are found on the coins of Greek fabric minted under Mithradates I. The caduceus, which is not uncommon on the Parthian money, would seem to belong to Nike or Eirene rather than to Hermes; and the Sphinx was probably associated with worship in general rather than the cultus of a special deity.

From this slight summary of facts it will appear that we have some grounds for supposing that the worship of some Greek deities, Pallas in particular, was officially recognized by the Parthians, and perhaps mingled by them with their other religion. Such worship would seem to have been more favoured in the reigns of Phraates IV. and Goterzes, which reigns, indeed, are notable for innovations of all kinds. It never took any deep root so far to the East.

The frequency with which the turreted female figures which represent the Greek cities of Eastern Asia appear, and the importance of the part which they play upon the tetradrachms, where they meet the King on equal terms, and he is proud to receive their homage, indicate the nature of the position held by the large cities subject to Parthia. The Parthian horsemen were never much at home within city walls, and were exceedingly unfitted to besiege fortified places. Seleucia, when it revolted, defied for years the whole force of the Parthian Empire when at its zenith. Hence throughout Parthian history the great cities of Babylonia, Susiana and the East enjoyed a qualified independence. They probably managed their internal affairs themselves, and were not interfered with so long as the tribute which was exacted from them was duly paid. Thus, in A.D. 40, at Seleucia, the Greek and Syrian elements of the population, combining together, overcame the Jews, and massacred 50,000 of them, apparently without the least interference from the Parthians, and without suffering any sort of punishment. It was the support afforded by these semi-independent Greek cities which enabled the Seleucid Syrian Kings to penetrate so easily and so far into Asia. To the Roman invaders they offered quite another reception; preferring the distant rule of a Phil-Hellenic barbarian to the ever-present tyranny of a Roman prætor.

With regard to the portraits of the Kings, one point is worthy of note. There is usually but slight difference between the representations of a king in the early years of his reign and those executed in his later years. His likeness was, so to speak, stereotyped as soon as he came to the throne. Then he became divine, and divine beings are above all changes. This rule, however, is not absolute. Pacorus II. is bearded on his later coins, beardless on his earlier. But most Parthian Kings were grown men when they came to the throne, and had probably made up their minds as to the best cut for a beard and the most becoming manner of wearing their hair, and any slight variation in the features, such as years produce, it would be quite beyond the power of a Parthian artist to portray.

Next to the types borne by the coins, come the inscriptions on them. Of these the most important part by far are the dates. The copper coins of the successors of Orodes often tell us in what year they were issued. The tetradrachms of the same princes give us still more precise information. For on them we find recorded not the year of issue only, but also the month. It has already been stated that the era used by the Parthians in dating is that of the Seleucidæ, which is reckoned from the 1st of October, 312 B.C. But as the length of this year was regulated, not by the sun, but by the moon, it is impossible to say with certainty and accuracy to what precise period the Seleucid years 20, 100, and so on belong; we can only make the general rule that the Seleucid year 100 corresponds to parts of 213/12 B.C., and so on with other dates. The Parthian year was divided into the twelve months, Dius, Apellæus, Audynæus, Peritius, Dystrus, Xanthicus, Artemisius, Dæsius, Panemus, Loïus, Gorpiæus, Hyperberetæus, of which the first corresponded roughly with October, and the rest in order with the succeeding months of our year. An intercalary month was inserted at intervals in order to bring back the months to their proper season. This was called Embolimus.

All the Parthian Kings save Orodes and Goterzes, until we reach the time of Pacorus II. and Vologeses III., used on their coins only the dynastic name of Arsaces. Writers say that all the kings took this name from veneration for the founder; but it is clear that Arsaces was only an official title like Pharaoh in Egypt, Cæsar and Augustus at Rome, and Czar at the present day in Russia. Every king had in addition a name peculiar to him, not a mere title like Euergetes and Philadelphus, such as the Ptolemies of Egypt took, but a real name. This they did not use on their coins perhaps because they issued coins in a purely official capacity, nor did they always use it in their dealings with foreign nations. But towards the end of the first century of the Christian era, the Parthian monarchy began to be split up among rival princes, each of whom claimed to be the true representative of the Arsacid line, and exercised the supreme power in a part of Western Asia. It was then that the custom arose for each monarch, in addition to the name of Arsaces, to place his more particular name upon some of his coins. I say *some*, because for a considerable time after the introduction of this custom it is the tetradrachms only which display the innovation, the drachms still reproducing in their blundered legend the dynastic title only. When this change does reach the drachms, the name which is found on them is in every case written, not in Greek, but in Pehlvi characters—a sign that the Greek tongue was no longer understood by the people.

The epithets and titles by which the Arsacid monarchs distinguish themselves are very varied. Indeed, we find the key to the arrangement of the pieces of the first thirteen kings in the variety of their legends, and particularly in their increasing length, and the number of titles they comprise. While the first monarch styles himself ΑΡΣΑΚΗΣ merely, or at most ΒΑΣΙΛΕΥΣ ΑΡΣΑΚΗΣ, the second adopts the style of ΒΑΣΙΛΕΥΣ ΜΕΓΑΣ, the fifth calls himself ΘΕΟΠΑΤΩΡ, the sixth, the first Mithradates, becomes ΒΑΣΙΛΕΥΣ ΒΑΣΙΛΕΩΝ and ΕΠΙΦΑΝΗΣ, while the second Phraates includes among his regular titles those of ΕΥΕΡΓΕΤΗΣ ΕΠΙΦΑΝΗΣ and ΦΙΛΕΛΛΗΝ. The string of titles goes on increasing until there is no more room to be found on the coin. Orodes fixed for himself and his successors the full royal style to the formula ΒΑΣΙΛΕΥΣ ΒΑΣΙΛΕΩΝ ΑΡΣΑΚΗΣ ΕΥΕΡΓΕΤΗΣ ΔΙΚΑΙΟΣ ΕΠΙΦΑΝΗΣ ΦΙΛΕΛΛΗΝ, which style is, with a few exceptions, regularly maintained to the end of the dynasty. It would be misleading to press too far the epithets selected by each monarch. Such terms as Philadelphus and Philopator certainly have a meaning, and are not applied at random; but others, like Theos, Nikator and Epiphanes, were probably adopted quite loosely, in most instances from the usage of contemporary Kings of Syria, Bactria or Armenia. Of ΒΑΣΙΛΕΥΣ ΜΕΓΑΣ and ΒΑΣΙΛΕΥΣ ΒΑΣΙΛΕΩΝ I have already spoken, and ΦΙΛΕΛΛΗΝ is the only interesting epithet which remains. This is introduced first in pieces struck by Greek cities under Parthian rule, and by degrees adopted on all coins. It shows us how desirous the Arsacid rulers were to conciliate to themselves the good opinion of the great Greek cities scattered through their domains, which probably furnished the greater part of their revenue. Having no civilization of their own, nor even a language at all suited to the intricacies of civilized life, the rude conquerors tried to adopt the language and the culture which had already, in the century which followed Alexander, made extensive inroads into Central Asia. The Greek tongue and Greek letters were to them what the French tongue and the French literature were to Frederick the Great of Prussia, or, to mention a still closer parallel, the Latin tongue and Latin literature to the Goths and Franks of the eighth century. I have given below a table of the titles assumed by the respective kings, and of the sources whence probably they are derived. The letters and monograms which appear sometimes on the obverse, but more often on the reverse of the coins, deserve serious attention. It has of late years become the custom to suppose that the monograms so usual on all coins of the Diadochi can be resolved into the names of mint-cities where they were issued. General Cunningham, in particular, has made elaborate efforts to read the monograms which appear on the Bactrian coins, and professes to have found in them the names of most of the cities of Bactria and the Panjab. As I have here no space to examine the method of this writer or discuss his results, I must content myself with referring to a very able article by M. Chabouillet, in the Revue Numismatique for 1867, page 392. I entirely agree with M. Chabouillet that there are but few cities, such as Odessus, Patræ, and Panormus, which are known to have placed on their coins a monogram to represent their names, and that in these cases the monogram was a sort of recognized symbol or arms of the town, and not a mere invention of the die-sinker. But to suppose that a monogram in the field of a coin usually represents the name of the mint whence it was issued, is to go altogether beyond the evidence.

M. Chabouillet is clearly right in saying that these monograms are usually merely the private mark of a magistrate or a contractor, and not intended to be decipherable to any one except himself. But even if they did contain the names of cities, it would be quite hopeless to attempt to read them, a monogram being a thing by nature most obscure and ambiguous. It can nearly always be read in three or four ways, and may often, by means of a little ingenuity, be made to represent anything the interpreter chooses.

I would divide the letters and monograms which occur on Parthian coins into four classes. The first class comprises those which occur on the obverse or head side of the coins of Phraates I. and Mithradates I., and of those princes only. On some of these an entire word, or at least great part of one, appears, and tempts one to a conjecture. NIΣAK may stand for Nisæa in Media, TAM for Tambrax, PA for Ragæ, ΣY for Syrinx: all these cities being situate within what were probably the territories of Phraates. The other letters and the monograms of this class I shall not attempt to interpret.

The second class occurs on the reverse of a small class of coins, usually given to Mithradates I., of distinctively Greek work and peculiar types. They are represented on Plate II. Nos. 1 and 2. These monograms are peculiarly distinct, and are three in number, 木, 𝕏𝕻 and 𝟬. These monograms, if they represent places, must signify three cities quite near together, and it may seem more than a fortunate coincidence that near Seleucia, by the Tigris, were three cities of Greek origin, bearing the names of Artamita, Charax and Phylace.

The third class comprises the letters and monograms which are found on the reverse of many coins, from the time of Phraates II. onwards to that of Vologeses I. Of these one, 𝔸, does certainly stand for a city, for it is found in connexion with the word ΠΟΛΙΣ. 𝕄, ΣΡ and ╠, which appear on the money of a succession of rulers, from the time of Mithradates II. onwards, probably also represent cities. But I am quite unable to prove to what city any one of the four belongs, and I fear to indulge in mere conjectures. Other monograms besides these occasionally occur, but none which can be interpreted with probability.

The fourth class consists of the first four letters of the Greek alphabet, which begin at the time of Goterzes, to be placed on the obverse of tetradrachms, behind the head of the monarch. The intent of these letters is quite obscure.

Even a superficial study of Parthian coins will bring to light the fact that they may be divided under every reign into two classes. The first class consists of the tetradrachms, and a certain number of copper coins, notably those bearing as type the figure or the head of a city. The second class consists of the drachms and obols, with the greater part of the copper coinage. The coins of the first class exhibit more care and a higher civilization than those of the second. The types exhibit higher art, and show more variety of idea, and the inscriptions are notably written with far greater clearness and correctness. On the drachms the Greek letters have become by the reign of Goterzes, or even before that, quite debased and unintelligible, being evidently executed by a die-sinker who could not read them. From the ordinary copper coins all legends have disappeared, and are replaced by a mere square or circle of dots. But the tetradrachms, and those pieces of copper which bear the head or figure of a city, can be read to the last, and were unquestionably produced in cities where the Greek tongue was by no means dead. This class of coins, too, bears, in all cases, dates according to the era of the Seleucidæ, while very few drachms of the Parthian Kings bear a date. The two series I have mentioned run parallel to one another, touching at but few points, so that it often is by no means easy to be sure with which tetradrachms some of the later drachms ought to be classed; the portrait is the only point in which the two series meet, and the notions of portraiture possessed by the artists of the tetradrachms differ entirely from those possessed by the artists of the drachms.

It has long been conjectured, and I think rightly, that the tetradrachms and civic copper were minted at some of the great Greek cities of Central Asia, such as Seleucia and Charax, while the drachms were the State coinage of the Parthian Empire, and struck wherever there was a Parthian garrison. On almost all the tetradrachms the King does not appear alone. He is usually in the act of receiving a palm or wreath from a female figure who wears a mural crown, and holds a sceptre or a cornucopiæ, and who clearly represents the mint city itself.

I have already mentioned the fact that some of the later drachms bear a legend which is not Greek. Two letters of this language occur on the coins of Sanabares, at the beginning of the Christian era, and about a century later the reigning monarchs' names in full appear so written with the title Malká or King. The resemblance of the characters in which these legends are written to the Sassanian-Persian letters attracted long ago the attention of the learned, and M. de Longpérier read them on that analogy. Similar characters are found on a host of smaller coins, which used to be called sub-Parthian, and which are of somewhat doubtful attribution. These I have entirely passed by, considering that the reading of them would be too uncertain, and not feeling myself competent to decide between the widely varying opinions of the Persian scholars in the matter. I treat, therefore, not of the coins of Parthian satraps, except where they bear the name of the Great King Arsaces, but of the regal coins of Parthia only.

IV. PARTHIAN COINAGE.

Arsaces I., II. Arsaces—Tiridates I.

Plate I. 1.   *Obv.* Head of Arsaces l. in helmet, round which is tied royal diadema.
      Rev. ΑΡΣΑΚΟΥ. Arsaces wearing helmet and cloak, seated r. on omphalos, holding bow.
                      Drachm. B.M. Wt. 59·2.

  I. 2.   [*Obv.* Similar.]
      Rev. ΒΑΣΙΛΕΩΣ ΑΡΣΑΚΟΥ. Same type; in ex. ᛉ.
                      Drachm. B.M. Wt. 55·4.

Plate I. 3.   *Obv.* Similar.
  Rev. ΒΑΣΙΛΕΩΣ ΜΕΓΑΛΟΥ ΑΡΣΑΚΟΥ. Same type.
  Drachm. Dr. Imhoof-Blumer. Wt. 54.

I. 4.   *Obv.* Similar.
  Rev. Same inscr. and type. At feet of king, torch.
  Drachm. B.M. Wt. 63·3.

I. 5.   *Obv.* Similar.
  Rev. Same inscr. and type.
  Obol. B.M. Wt. 9·4

Varieties of No. 3 :—In field l. of rev. Θ (B.M.). In ex. of rev. ⅚ (P.O.).

I have not divided the coins which I attribute to Tiridates from those which I give to Arsaces, because it is impossible to separate finally the former from the latter class. The portrait presented on all five coins is that of the founder of the dynasty; but it is scarcely to be believed that the first Arsaces should, in his short reign of two years, have adopted on his coins first the title of King, and then that of Great King. As it was Tiridates who first extended the bounds of the Parthian Empire beyond the limits of Parthia proper, and met the Kings of Syria in open battle, I regard it as almost certain that Nos. 3, 4 and 5 of the plate were issued by him, and that he retained from a motive of respect his brother's portrait on all his coins. It is indeed by no means impossible that No. 2 may also have been struck by Tiridates, and No. 1, which is of great rarity, may be the only coin issued by Arsaces himself. But certainty is not attainable in this as in many other questions of Parthian numismatics.

ARSACES III.   ARTABANUS I.

Plate I. 6.   *Obv.* Head of Artabanus l. diademed : border of reels and beads.
  Rev. ΒΑΣΙΛΕΩΣ ΜΕΓΑΛΟΥ ΑΡΣΑΚΟΥ. Arsaces seated r. on omphalos.
  Drachm. B.M. Wt. 55·6.

7.   As last.
  Obol. B.M. Wt. 9.

8.   *Obv.* As last.
  Rev. Same inscr. Horse r. trotting.
  B.M. Æ ·65.

The difficulty of arranging the coins of the first thirteen Arsacidæ is proverbial. As I have departed somewhat widely from the wisdom of my predecessors, I must give from time to time a sketch of my reasons for my attributions. Therefore I devote two brief discussions, one under Phraates I., one under Mithradates III., to the justification of the new order.

Arsaces IV. Phraapates.

Plate I. 9. *Obv.* Head of Phraapates l., diademed.
Rev. ΒΑΣΙΛΕΩΣ ΜΕΓΑΛΟΥ ΑΡΣΑΚΟΥ ΦΙΛΑΔΕΛΦΟΥ. Arsaces seated r. on omphalos.
Drachm. B.M. Wt. 59.

10. *Obv.* As last; behind Ȧ.
Rev. Same legend with ΦΙΛΕΛΛΗΝΟΣ added. Same type; in ex. ΕΚΡ (year 125).
Drachm. B.M. Wt. 61.

11. *Obv.* As last.
Rev. ΒΑΣΙΛΕΩΣ ΜΕΓΑΛΟΥ ΑΡΣΑΚΟΥ. Horse r. trotting.
B.M. Æ ·75.

Varieties:—Of No. 9, on obv. ΡΑ (B.M). Of No. 11, on obv. mon. of No. 10; rev. Horse's head (P.O.).

The attribution of the coins of Phraapates is rendered certain by the occurrence of a date, the year 125 of the Seleucid era, or B.C. 188–7. Of the title Philadelphus we can say nothing, because we are totally ignorant of his relations to his predecessors, contemporaries and successors. The important epithet Philhellen here first occurs, and was evidently conferred upon the king by some Greek city, grateful for favours past or to come. But its occurrence here is exceptional; the Parthian kings had probably scarcely learnt as yet the importance of the favour of their Greek subjects.

Arsaces V. Phraates I.

Plate I. 12. *Obv.* Head of Phraates r. diademed: border of reels and beads.
Rev. ΒΑΣΙΛΕΩΣ ΑΡΣΑΚΟΥ. Apollo seated l. on omphalos, holds bow and arrow; to l. mon. Ⓜ, in ex. ΒΑ: border of dots.
Tetradrachm. Berlin. Wt. 251·5.

13. *Obv.* Head of Phraates l., beard thicker; behind ΤΑΜ.
Rev. ΒΑΣΙΛΕΩΣ ΜΕΓΑΛΟΥ ΑΡΣΑΚΟΥ ΘΕΟΠΑΤΟΡΟΣ. Arsaces seated r. on omphalos.
Drachm. B.M. Wt. 64.

14. As last, no mint-letters.
Obol. B.M. Wt. 9.

15. *Obv.* As last.
Rev. ΒΑΣΙΛΕΩΣ ΜΕΓΑΛΟΥ ΑΡΣΑΚΟΥ. Horse r. trotting.
B.M. Æ ·6.

16. *Obv.* As last.
Rev. As last. ΘΕΟΠΑΤΟΡΟΣ added to legend.
B.M. Æ ·6.

Varieties of No. 13:—On obv. mint-letters ΝΙΣΑΚ·; Ⓡ, Α (B.M.); ΣΥΡ; ΜΗ (P.O.). Of No. 16, type of rev. Elephant, r.

I have adopted, after some hesitation, Dr. von Sallet's opinion as to the unique tetradrachm, chiefly on the grounds of iconography. I do not think it can be disputed that if
this coin belong to any Parthian King, it must belong to him who issued the drachm No. 13,
which I shall presently prove to belong to Phraates. And it seems improbable that a piece
bearing the name Arsaces should belong to any but a Parthian King. The only other visible
possibility is, that it was issued by one of the Arsacid monarchs of Armenia; but there is
no ground for Von Prokesch-Osten's conjecture, who gives it to Demetrius II. of Syria.
If the piece be Parthian, it is quite exceptional, and must issue from a mint which, having
only just ceased to strike money for the Seleucid Kings, and falling into the power of the
Parthians, transferred type and style to the conqueror. Of the letters and monogram I can
give no account. I have above conjectured the mint letters which appear on drachms of this
King to represent Nisæa, Tambrax, Rhagæ, and Syrinx, with other uncertain cities.

The coins of Tiridates are fairly certain; so are those of Mithradates I. Between
these two Kings there intervene Artabanus I., Phraapates, and Phraates I. Now the
coins which precede Mithradates are marked off from those which follow him by one clear
distinguishing mark; in the former class the King is always seated on the omphalos of
Apollo, in the latter always on a throne with four legs and a back. The legends also of the
former class are shorter and simpler. The pre-Mithradatic class of coins presents us with
three distinct types of heads (besides that appropriated to the first and second Arsaces) to
correspond to Artabanus, Phraapates, and Phraates. It only remains to settle which portrait
belongs to which King. The coin which bears the date of the Seleucid era 125, a date
which falls in the middle of the reign of Phraapates, leaves us no doubt as to the attribution of the class of coins which bear the same head as appears on the dated coin (Plate I.
9–11). My attribution of the coins (12-16) to Phraates is supported by weighty reasons.
The fabric of these pieces is closely like the fabric of Mithradates' coins; the hair of the
two Kings is alike. There are two reasons better still. With the coins which I give to
Phraates goes the earliest Parthian tetradrachm. Tetradrachms of Mithradates are not uncommon, and it is more reasonable to suppose that these coins were introduced by the predecessor of Mithradates, and continued by him, rather than that they were introduced by
some earlier prince, and then for a time discontinued. Finally, the monograms and names of
mint cities which appear on the set of coins which I am discussing, are continued under
Mithradates. Only Mithradates and the King who issued these coins adopted the custom
of placing the name of the mint on the obverse of their pieces, behind the royal effigy;
therefore the conclusion is almost irresistible that Mithradates and the King who issued these
coins reigned consecutively; in other words, that these coins were issued by Phraates. Hitherto
they have usually been ascribed to Artabanus I.

The remaining portrait belongs to Artabanus.

If the series of coins be arranged as I have arranged them, and the eye be passed from
one to the other in regular order, a gradual development of style will be observed throughout.

And one other interesting indication will appear. There is a peculiar style of border, commonly called the reel and bead border, which I have ascertained from a study of the coins of the Seleucidæ to appear first in Syria nearly about the year B.C. 225-4, just before the time of Antiochus the Great. This peculiar border appears in a pronounced manner on the coins which I attribute to Artabanus I., who was contemporary with Antiochus. In the time of Phraapates it had already fallen out of use; though, as we shall see, Mithradates revived it in a few of his coins, but not on his usual drachms, which, like the coins which I give to Phraates, have the usual border of dots.

ARSACES VI. MITHRADATES I.

(a). With diadem. Title—βασιλεὺς μέγας.

Plate I. 17. *Obv.* Head of Mithradates l. diademed.

Rev. ΒΑΣΙΛΕΩΣ ΜΕΓΑΛΟΥ ΑΡΣΑΚΟΥ ΕΠΙΦΑΝΟΥΣ. Arsaces I. seated r. on omphalos holding bow; behind Ⱥ, to r. palm.

Tetradrachm. Paris.

18. As last, without monogram (ruder style).

Tetradrachm. Berlin. Wt. 227·6.

19. As last, no monogram or palm.

Drachm. B.M. Wt. 61.

20. *Obv.* As last; behind MI.

Rev. Same inscription. Bow in case and arrows.

B.M. Æ ·55.

21. *Obv.* As last, no mint-letters.

Rev. Same inscription. Nike r. holding wreath and palm.

B.M. Æ ·45.

22. *Obv.* As last, behind A.

Rev. Same inscription. Horse's head r.

B.M. Æ ·7.

Varieties:—Of No. 17, on rev. TY (Berlin). Of No. 19, on obv. ⨳, ⨳, ⨳, ⨳ and other monograms; on rev. A (B.M.), ⨳, etc. Of Nos. 21, 22, types of copper, horse r , monograms of copper on obv. ⨳; on rev. MI.

(β.) With diadem. Title—βασιλεὺς βασιλέων.

Plate I. 23. *Obv.* Head of Mithradates l. diademed.

Rev. ΒΑΣΙΛΕΩΣ ΒΑΣΙΛΕΩΝ ΜΕΓΑΛΟΥ ΑΡΣΑΚΟΥ ΕΠΙΦΑΝΟΥΣ. Arsaces seated r. on *throne* holding bow.

Drachm. B.M. Wt. 65·4.

Plate I. 24.　*Obv.* As last; behind ᴹᴵᖇ.
　　　　　　　　Rev. Same inscr., Horse's head r.

B.M.　Æ ·65.

Varieties:—Types of copper, Pegasus r., bow in case; mint-letters on copper MI.

(γ). With helmet.　Title—*βασιλεὺς βασιλέων.*

25.　*Obv.* Head of Mithradates l. wearing helmet, on the side of which, star; outside it, diadem.
　　　Rev. ΒΑΣΙΛΕΩΣ ΒΑΣΙΛΕΩΝ ΜΕΓΑΛΟΥ ΑΡΣΑΚΟΥ ΕΠΙΦΑΝΟΥΣ.　Arsaces seated
　　　r. on *throne* holding bow.

Drachm.　B.M.　Wt. 63·4.

26.　As last.

Drachm.　B.M.　Wt. 64·1.

27.　*Obv.* Similar head; behind ᴱᖇ.
　　　Rev. Same inscr.　Nike r. holding wreath and palm.

B.M.　Æ ·6.

Varieties:—Types of copper, Pegasus r., club.

(δ). With helmet.　Title—*εὐεργέτης δικαιὸς φιλέλλην.*

28.　*Obv.* Head of Mithradates? l. wearing helmet bound with diadem.
　　　Rev. ΒΑΣΙΛΕΩΣ ΒΑΣΙΛΕΩΝ ΑΡΣΑΚΟΥ ΕΥΕΡΓΕΤΟΥ ΔΙΚΑΙΟΥ ΚΑΙ ΦΙΛΕΛΛΗΝΟΣ.
　　　Arsaces seated r. on throne holding bow.

Drachm.　B.M.　Wt. 63.

(ε). GREEK FABRIC.　Doubtful class.

Plate II. 1.　*Obv.* Head of a King r. diad.: border of reels and beads.
　　　　　　Rev. ΒΑΣΙΛΕΩΣ ΜΕΓΑΛΟΥ ΑΡΣΑΚΟΥ ΦΙΛΕΛΛΗΝΟΣ.　Herakles l. holding winecup
　　　　　　and club; over arm lion's skin; in field l. 𝍓; in ex. ΓΟΡ (year 173).

Tetradrachm.　B.M.　Wt. 246·4.

2.　*Obv.* As last.
　　　Rev. ΒΑΣΙΛΕΩΣ ΜΕΓΑΛΟΥ ΑΡΣΑΚΟΥ.　Zeus seated l. holding eagle and sceptre, 𝍓
　　　and ΓΟΡ as before.

Drachm.　B.M.　Wt. 51·4.

Varieties:—Of No. 1, rev. Φ ΓΟΡ, ΔΟΡ, ΧΡ (two latter B.M.).　Of No. 6, rev. ΧΡ (B.M.) and Ⅹ (P.O.).

(ζ). BACTRIAN ISSUE?　Doubtful class.

Plate II. 3.　*Obv.* Head of a King r. diademed: border of reels and beads.
　　　　　　Rev. ΒΑΣΙΛΕΩΣ ΜΕΓΑΛΟΥ ΑΡΣΑΚΟΥ.　Arsaces seated r.
　　　　　　　　　　　Drachm.　B.M.　Wt. 62·8.

Plate II. 4. *Obv.* Same head; no border.
        Rev. ΒΑΣΙΛΕΩΣ ΜΕΓΑΛΟΥ ΑΡΣΑΚΟΥ. The Dioscuri on horseback charging r.

                B.M. Æ 1·1.

    5. *Obv.* [As last].
        Rev. Same inscr. Elephant r.

                B.M. Æ 1·1.

    6. *Obv.* As last.
        Rev. Inscr. obscure. Nike in quadriga r.

                B.M. Æ ·75.

    7. *Obv.* Head of King r. diad.
        Rev. ΒΑΣΙΛΕΩΣ ΜΕΓΑΛΟΥ ΑΡΣΑΚΟΥ. Head of a king r. with a long beard, in
        Scythian helmet.

          Obol. B.M. Wt. 10·2.

Varieties:—Of Nos. 4–6, types of copper, bow in case, horse's head r., fly, Nike r. holding wreath (all
B.M.). Of No. 7, same types and legend in copper (Æ ·65, B.M.).

The attribution of classes *a*, *β*, *γ* is fairly certain. Some writers have indeed supposed
that the head of class *a*, usually with short round beard, is not the same as the head of
class *β* with long beard. But Mithradates had a long reign, and many changes may have
been made in the coinage. When he adopted the title βασιλεὺς βασιλέων, he allowed an
entirely fresh portrait of himself to appear on his coins, showing him as a more mature man.
I think that no one denies the head wearing helmet of class *γ* to be the same as the diademed
head of class *β*. Of this helmet I have spoken above.

It is difficult to believe that the coins of class δ were issued by this King. The titles
εὐεργέτης and δικαιὸς do not again appear on the Parthian coins for a long while to come,
and the portrait of the King presents some modification. I have little doubt that these pieces
were struck after the death of Mithradates, either during an interregnum, or by some prince
too modest to wish to place his own effigy on his coins. But to attempt to define their period
more closely would be nothing but guess-work; so that they are best placed last among the
coins of Mithradates. The title εὐεργέτης was introduced by Ptolemy III. of Egypt; that
of δικαιὸς by Agathocles of Bactria. Both titles, therefore, are as early as the third century
B.C., and there is no reason why Mithradates should not have adopted them as well as any of
his successors.

The silver coins composing class ε have caused a great deal of discussion. Their date is
fortunately fixed by the letters in their exergues to B.C. 140–138, a period which well agrees
with the general style of the coins. This period certainly falls within the reign of Mithradates; but, on the other hand, the head of the coins differs decidedly from the usual head of
the great Parthian. Count von Prokesch-Osten has maintained that the pieces belong to
Valarsaces, whom, according to Moses of Chorene, Mithradates established as King in Armenia,

and Western Asia generally. This is possible, but we must not forget that we have here only the very worthless testimony of Moses for the existence of Valarsaces, and further that this testimony is contradicted by the language of Strabo. The most probable supposition is that these coins were issued by some Greek cities, in special honour of Mithradates—some cities which he had spared after conquering them, or which had voluntarily submitted to him. The portrait of the King is indeed varied; but the general outlines are not irreconcilable, and we must make allowance for the superiority of Greek work. There seems to be some reason for supposing all these pieces to have been issued in or near Babylonia, for I have above shown that the mint-monograms on them seem to point to a group of cities near Charax. The type of Herakles is adopted in compliment to the Parthian legend which represented the Greek hero as the ancestor of their race.

Class ζ is composed of coins usually given to a very early Arsacid. I have one reason for removing them hither which seems to me of the greatest weight. The type of No. 4 is closely, even slavishly, copied from the coins of the great Eucratides, King of Bactria. The resemblance is so close, and it is so certain that a Parthian King would adopt a Greek type, not a Greek a Parthian type, that I regard it as entirely certain that these coins were issued while Eucratides was King of Bactria. Now Justin states clearly that Eucratides began his reign at the same time as Mithradates of Parthia. The coins of class ζ then fall within the reign of Mithradates. The portrait on the first four, Nos. 3-6, does not seem to be that of Mithradates, although there is a certain distant resemblance; but I am inclined to think that the second portrait on No. 7, that in the Scythian head-dress, represents Mithradates. I should have been inclined to suppose that the first portrait was that of Valarsaces, but that, according to our accounts, Valarsaces ruled in the western part of Parthia, while these coins have an unmistakably Bactrian tinge. They may have been issued by Bacasis, whom Mithradates set over Media, or by some other of his many satraps.

ARSACES VII. PHRAATES II.

Plate II.   8.   *Obv.* Head of Phraates l. diademed.

         Rev. ΒΑΣΙΛΕΩΣ ΜΕΓΑΛΟΥ ΑΡΣΑΚΟΥ ΘΕΟΠΑΤΟΡΟΣ ΕΥΕΡΓΕΤΟΥ ΕΠΙΦΑ-ΝΟΥΣ ΦΙΛΕΛΛΗΝΟΣ. Arsaces seated r. on throne holding bow; above ⋈ .

Tetradrachm.   B.M.   Wt. 240·7.

      9.   *Obv.* As last.

         Rev. ΒΑΣΙΛΕΩΣ ΜΕΓΑΛΟΥ ΑΡΣΑΚΟΥ ΘΕΟΠΑΤΟΡΟΣ ΕΥΕΡΓΕΤΟΥ. Arsaces seated r.

Drachm.   B.M.   Wt. 60·3.

    10.   *Obv.* As last.

         Rev. Same inscription. Horse trotting r.

B.M.   Æ ·65.

Plate II. 11. *Obv.* As last.

    Rev. Same inscription. Arsaces seated r.: to r. ΚΑΤΑΣΤΡΑΤΕΙΑ written downwards.

        Drachm. B.M. Wt. 55·5.

    12. (*Obv.* As last).

    Rev. As last, but legend to r. ΤΡΑΞΙΑΝΗ.

        Drachm. B.M. Wt. 51·9.

Varieties:—Of No. 8, on rev. various monograms ⋈, B, etc. (P.O.). Of No. 11, legend ΓΟΡΟΥ ΚΑΤΑΣΤΡΑΤΕΙΑ (Paris). Of No. 12, legend ΜΑΡΓΙΑΝΗ (Berlin). Of No. 10, type of copper, elephant r. (B.M.); legend of copper as that of tetradrachms, type horse (P.O.).

The attribution of these coins is, I believe, undisputed. The title θεοπατώρ well suits Phraates, as we have reason to suppose, from the words of Trogus Pompeius, that Mithradates his father assumed the title θεός. The three legends Καταστρατεῖα, Μαργιανή and Τραξιανή are as yet unexplained. The word ΓΟΡΟΥ, in connexion with the first of these, is vouched for by good authority; otherwise I should have been inclined to suppose it the mere remains of a previous striking, such remains being on Parthian drachms as much the rule as the exception. The word Καταστρατεῖα does not occur in the lexicons, and is very doubtful Greek, if we attach to it the meaning of expedition, the particle κατα being quite superfluous. Μαργιανή, which Dr. von Sallet first found on a coin, is the undoubted name of a province. Τραξιανή must also from its form be a geographical name, although I do not find it in the Geographers. I am therefore tempted to believe that Καταστρατεῖα also must be a geographical term, the name of some small town or station probably founded by Phraates or his predecessor.

ARSACES VIII. ARTABANUS II.

Plate II. 13. *Obv.* Head of Artabanus l. wearing helmet with horn at side and foreparts of stags around; bound round it diadem.

    Rev. ΒΑΣΙΛΕΩΣ ΜΕΓΑΛΟΥ ΑΡΣΑΚΟΥ ΘΕΟΠΑΤΟΡΟΣ ΝΙΚΑΤΟΡΟΣ. Arsaces seated r.

        Drachm. B.M. Wt. 63·7.

    14. *Obv.* As last.

    Rev. Same inscr. Nike r. with wreath and palm.

        B.M. Æ ·6.

    15. *Obv.* As last.

    Rev. Same inscr. Club.

        B.M. Æ ·5.

Varieties:—Type of copper, Pegasus r. (B.M.).

I postpone the question of the attribution of these coins until I come to the coins of Mithradates III., where I annex a short dissertation. The only matter which calls for remark is the very peculiar form of the helmet of this and the succeeding king.

Himerus.

Plate II. 16.   *Obv.* Head of Himerus r. slightly bearded, wearing diadem.
   Rev. ΒΑΣΙΛΕΩΣ ΜΕΓΑΛΟΥ ΑΡΣΑΚΟΥ ΝΙΚΗΦΟΡΟΥ. Nike l. holding wreath and
   palm; in ex. ΘΠΡ (year 189).

       Drachm.   P.O.   Wt. 56·6.

  I have already spoken of the place held by Himerus in Parthian history, and have shown
that he was reckoned a king, and that he was put down in the early part of the reign of
Mithradates II.   Both these facts, which are made known to us by the writers, are further
confirmed by this unique and interesting coin first published by Count von Prokesch-Osten.
The date proves that it was struck in the first year of the reign of Mithradates II., and so
makes the attribution certain, while the style of the head corresponds very well with what
we know as regards both the age and the character of Himerus.   Its type is that of a man
of about twenty years of age, and of a sensual and callous turn.   The likeness to the head of
young Nero is striking.   As it was the first act of Molon and of Timarchus, when they
revolted against the Seleucid kings, to strike money bearing their own types, so we need
not be surprised that their example was followed under parallel circumstances by this young
Hyrcanian Greek.

Arsaces IX. Mithradates II.

(a). With diadem.

Plate II. 17.   *Obv.* Head of Mithradates l. diad.
   Rev. ΒΑΣΙΛΕΩΣ ΜΕΓΑΛΟΥ ΑΡΣΑΚΟΥ ΕΥΕΡΓΕΤΟΥ ΕΠΙΦΑΝΟΥΣ ΚΑΙ ΦΙΛ-
   ΕΛΛΗΝΟΣ. Arsaces seated r. on throne holding bow; above ᛉ.

      Tetradrachm.   B.M.   Wt. 199·2.

  18.   *Obv.* As last.
   Rev. Same inscr. without ΚΑΙ. Same type; in field r. ▧.

      Drachm.   B.M.   Wt. 62·2.

  Varieties of No. 18, monograms on rev. ⅀Ρ, ┌Ρ, ₳ (B.M.), ᴮᴹ (P.O.).   Types of copper, Pegasus, horse
r., horse's head r., with monograms ┌Ρ or ₳ (B.M.).

(β). With helmet.

  19.   *Obv.* Head of Mithradates l. in helmet with horn at side and foreparts of stags around.
   Rev. ΒΑΣΙΛΕΩΣ ΜΕΓΑΛΟΥ ΑΡΣΑΚΟΥ ΘΕΟΥ ΕΥΕΡΓΕΤΟΥ ΕΠΙΦΑΝΟΥΣ ΦΙΛ-
   ΕΛΛΗΝΟΣ. Mithradates seated l. holding eagle and sceptre; behind, a City, wearing
   mural crown and holding sceptre, crowning him.

      Tetradrachm.   P.O.   Wt. 231·6.

Plate II. 20. *Obv.* As last.

> *Rev.* Same inscr. without ΘΕΟΥ. Arsaces seated r.; to l. 𝕏.
> *Drachm.* B.M. Wt. 61·2.

21. As last, monogram 𝚺𝚸.

> *Drachm.* B.M. Wt. 61·4.

22. *Obv.* As last, no monogram.
> *Rev.* Same inscr., Horse r.
>
> B.M. Æ ·65.

Varieties:—Of Nos. 20–21, monograms on rev. 𝖬, 𝕭, etc. (B.M.). Of No. 22, type of copper, horse's head r.

(γ). Doubtful class.

23. *Obv.* Head of a King l. in helmet, on the side of which a trefoil ornament, round it diadem.
> *Rev.* ΒΑΣΙΛΕΩΣ ΜΕΓΑΛΟΥ ΑΡΣΑΚΟΥ ΕΥΕΡΓΕΤΟΥ ΕΠΙΦΑΝΟΥΣ ΦΙΛΕΛΛΗΝΟΣ.
> Arsaces seated r.
> *Drachm.* B.M. Wt. 57·3.

24. *Obv.* Head of a King l. in helmet, on the side of which a trefoil ornament, and round the edge balls; behind, anchor.
> *Rev.* As last.
> *Drachm.* B.M. Wt. 63.

Question of attribution postponed. It is interesting to note in No. 19 the assumption of the title θεός, a title first taken in Asia, I believe, by Antiochus II. The type also of this coin presents an interesting innovation. The reigning King henceforward usually takes, on tetradrachms, the place of the founder of the dynasty, and appears either in the attitude of Zeus Aëtophoros of the coins of Alexander the Great, or, more frequently, in the act of receiving a wreath or a palm from a city personified in female form. The founder keeps his place on the drachms.

Arsaces X. Sinatroces.

Plate III. 1. *Obv.* Head of Sinatroces l. in helmet, on the side of which star, bound with diadem.
> *Rev.* ΒΑΣΙΛΕΩΣ ΜΕΓΑΛΟΥ ΑΡΣΑΚΟΥ ΑΥΤΟΚΡΑΤΟΡΟΣ ΦΙΛΟΠΑΤΟΡΟΣ ΕΠΙ-
> ΦΑΝΟΥΣ ΦΙΛΕΛΛΗΝΟΣ. Arsaces I. seated r. on throne holding bow; in front A.
> *Tetradrachm.* Berlin. Wt. 208·5.

2. *Obv.* As last.
> *Rev.* As last, without A.
> *Drachm.* B.M. Wt. 62·8.

3. *Obv.* As last.
> *Rev.* Same inscr. Horse's head r.
> B.M. Æ ·55.

Variety:—type of copper, horse r.

These coins have usually been attributed to Artabanus II.; for my reasons for transposing them see further on. The title αὐτοκρατώρ appears here for the first time on Parthian coins, and only once again, on a coin given to Phraates IV. It was most probably adopted by Sinatroces, who was a contemporary of Sulla's great conquests in the East, as the equivalent of the Roman *Dictator*.

Arsaces X. Phraates III.

(a). Full-face.

Plate III. 4. *Obv.* Head of Phraates, facing, diad.
   Rev. ΒΑΣΙΛΕΩΣ ΜΕΓΑΛΟΥ ΑΡΣΑΚΟΥ ΘΕΟΠΑΤΟΡΟΣ ΕΥΕΡΓΕΤΟΥ ΕΠΙΦΑ-
   ΝΟΥΣ ΦΙΛΕΛΛΗΝΟΣ. Arsaces seated r.; in front 𝖠.
      Drachm. B.M. Wt. 62·8.

  5. *Obv.* As last.
   Rev. Same inscr., ΚΑΙ before ΦΙΛΕΛΛΗΝΟΣ. Horse r. trotting.
      B.M. Æ ·7.

  6. *Obv.* As last.
   Rev. Same inscription. Elephant r.
      Æ ·5.

Varieties of No. 4, ΚΑΙ sometimes inserted in inscriptions before the last word, the monograms 𝚺𝐏, 𝖄, etc., appear. Type of copper, Nike r. (B.M.).

(β). Side-face.

  7. *Obv.* Head of Phraates l., diad.
   Rev. ΒΑΣΙΛΕΩΣ ΜΕΓΑΛΟΥ ΑΡΣΑΚΟΥ ΦΙΛΟΠΑΤΟΡΟΣ ΕΥΕΡΓΕΤΟΥ ΕΠΙΦΑ-
   ΝΟΥΣ ΦΙΛΕΛΛΗΝΟΣ. Arsaces I. seated r. on throne, holding bow; in front 𝖡𝖠⁄𝖹.
      Tetradrachm. P.O. Wt. 208·1.

  8. *Obv.* As last.
   Rev. Same inscr. Arsaces seated r., in front 𝖄.
      Drachm. B.M. Wt. 62.

  9. *Obv.* Same head; behind, Nike placing wreath on it.
   Rev. Same inscr. Horse r. trotting.
      B.M. Æ ·7

  10. As last, type, Nike r.
      B.M. Æ ·55.

Varieties:—Of No. 7, monogram on rev. ₣ (Paris and P.O.), other monograms. Of No. 8, monograms on rev. 𝖠, 𝖯𝖡, 𝖠, ΚΑΙ before last word of legend (B.M.).

On these coins Nike makes her first appearance in connexion with the head of the reigning monarch. This somewhat barbarous idea would seem to be of Parthian origin; at least I am not aware of any previous coins from which it could be copied. The custom is kept up by the later Parthian monarchs, and adopted on some of the copper pieces of Augustus.

ARSACES XI. MITHRADATES III.

Plate III. 11. *Obv.* Head of Mithradates l. diad., the neck-ornament of beads with clasp in front.

Rev. ΒΑΣΙΛΕΩΣ ΜΕΓΑΛΟΥ ΑΡΣΑΚΟΥ ΕΠΙΦΑΝΟΥΣ ΔΙΚΑΙΟΥ ΘΕΟΥ ΕΥΠΑ-ΤΟΡΟΣ ΚΑΙ ΦΙΛΕΛΛΗΝΟΣ. Arsaces seated r.; in front Ḡ.

Drachm. B.M. Wt. 58.

12. *Obv.* As last.
Rev. Same inscr. without ΚΑΙ. Horse r. standing.

B.M. Æ ·7.

13. *Obv.* Same head; behind, star.
Rev. ΒΑΣΙΛΕΩΣ ΒΑΣΙΛΕΩΝ ΑΡΣΑΚΟΥ ΜΕΓΑΛΟΥ ΔΙΚΑΙΟΥ ΕΠΙΦΑΝΟΥΣ ΘΕΟΥ ΕΥΠΑΤΟΡΟΣ ΦΙΛΕΛΛΗΝΟΣ. Elephant r.

B.M. Æ ·65.

14. As last, type, elephant's head r.

B.M. Æ ·5.

Varieties :—Of the drachm No. 11 there are numerous varieties, not of type, but of legend. Of these the principal are, the legend of No. 13, and the remarkable variant ΒΑΣΙΛΕΥΟΝΤΟΣ ΒΑΣΙΛΕΩΝ ΑΡΣΑΚΟΥ ΕΥΠΑΤΟΡΟΣ ΔΙΚΑΙΟΥ ΕΠΙΦΑΝΟΥΣ ΚΑΙ ΦΙΛΕΛΛΗΝΟΣ, mint ΣḠ (B.M.). The monograms on these drachms are Ⱥ, Κ, ⅏ (all B.M.) and others. Varieties of No. 12, type of rev. horse's head r. (B.M.). Of 13–14 type of rev. Pegasus r. with or without monogram Ḡ (B.M.).

If these coins were issued by Greek cities or princes, it would be interesting to inquire what was the occasion of the introduction of the participle βασιλεύων, or the force attached to it. But it seems probable that among the barbarous Parthians it is introduced as a mere variety in expression, with no meaning different from that contained in βασιλέως. We have in the same way the word τυραννοῦντος on the pieces of the barbarous king Heraüs (Num. Chron. N.S. vol. xiv. p. 161). Like modern barbarians, those of old liked to add to the length of words, merely for the sake of having them long. On the pieces of Mithradates generally, and many of those of Orodes, the legend pursues a devious course all about the coin, so that it sometimes takes several minutes to discover where words begin and where they end. It is exceedingly difficult to put into exact form the considerations which have influenced me in my arrangement of the coins of the VIII.–XI. Arsaces, and those which I give to the early part of the reign of Orodes. The varieties of style and treatment which lead the eye cannot be fully communicated even by word of mouth, far less by writing. However the attempt must be made.

I have above observed that king Mnaskires has to be ignominiously expelled from the list of monarchs, into which, indeed, he ought never to have been admitted, and that we have no reason to suppose that any one intervenes between Mithradates the Second and Sinatroces, or if any one, it was probably only a temporary usurper. The number of kings who reigned in the period between Mithradates and Orodes is thus reduced from five to four. The first point that seemed clear to me was, that the coins usually attributed to Artabanus II., Plate III. 1–3, belong really to a later date. Of this the lettering and the type of the reverse, both the very surest of signs, convinced me. At first sight the title αὐτοκράτωρ adopted on them would seem to mark them out as issued by a monarch contemporary with Tryphon of Syria, who used on his money the style αὐτοκράτωρ, and who reigned about B.C. 140. This is no doubt the reason for which Tryphon's contemporary, Artabanus II., has been hitherto selected as the issuer of these coins. But it must be remembered that αὐτοκράτωρ is the equivalent of the Roman word Dictator. Sulla of Rome, whose name was well known to all the kings of the East, became Roman Dictator in the year B.C. 81. Sinatroces ascended the Parthian throne five years later. It seems then very natural that Sinatroces should have assumed the title αὐτοκράτωρ in rivalry of Sulla, and issued the present set of coins. To this argument we may add another.

The head on the coins Pl. III. 1–3 is certainly that of a very aged man, and, if it is not of Artabanus, must be of Sinatroces, whom we know from Lucian to have come to the throne at an advanced age. This point being fixed, all the mass of coins after the reign of Phraates II. and before that of Orodes fall into two classes, of which the class which bear a head with long beard fall before, those which bear a head with short beard fall after the reign of Sinatroces. To begin with the former class. There can, I think, be no doubt whatever that the diademed head of Pl. II. 18 is the same portrait as the head in helmet of Pl. II. 20, and as the legend is substantially the same, these coins must have belonged to the same monarch, who is doubtless the illustrious Mithradates II. With these go the tetradrachms, Pl. II. 17, 19, the latter of which, with its reading θεοῦ, adds to the probability of my arrangement, Mithradates being more likely than any prince of his time to assume divinity. There are left of the long-bearded type of coins three sets, all of which bear heads similar to, but not identical with, that of Mithradates. See Pl. II. 13, 23, 24. No. 13 bears the titles θεοπάτωρ and νικατώρ, the former of which is appropriate to Artabanus II. as son of the first Mithradates, the latter to him as contemporary of Demetrius Nicator of Syria. The coinage represented by No. 13 is plentiful and of good metal. For all these reasons it seems to me probable that it should be attributed to Artabanus II. In Nos. 23 and 24 the helmet of Mithradates and Artabanus is repeated with a variety, a trefoil instead of a horn at the side, and not adorned with the foreparts of stags. The portrait on these is also degraded, and the metal usually debased. They represent either the later coinage of Mithradates II. issued at out-of-the-way mints and during a disturbed part of his reign, or else the money of some ephemeral usurper.

The class of coins with short beard remains to be treated of. Writers are agreed that the full-face coins Nos. 4–6 are of Phraátes III., and I accept their opinion, although the reason they give, that Phraates was joint ruler with his father, and that the heir to the throne is always thus represented, breaks down entirely. For in the first place, we do not know that Phraates was joint ruler with his father; but secondly, Pacorus, who certainly was joint ruler, is always represented side-face. Notwithstanding this, the attribution seems a sound one. And the head which is turned to the left on coins Nos. 7–10 is the same as that represented full-face on Nos. 4–6. These sets of coins then are both of the same king; the slight variety in the legend $\theta\epsilon o\pi\alpha\tau\omega\rho$ and $\phi\iota\lambda o\pi\alpha\tau\omega\rho$ notwithstanding. And that this king is Phraates there can be scarcely a doubt. The remaining coins belong partly to Mithradates III. and partly to the early years of the reign of Orodes, before he had adopted a fixed legend. Two main differences divide the coins of these two princes. The first is of legend; Mithradates styling himself $\theta\epsilon o\varsigma$ $\epsilon\upsilon\pi\alpha\tau\omega\rho$, and Orodes $\phi\iota\lambda o\pi\alpha\tau\omega\rho$. These epithets perhaps are not very appropriate, seeing that the two combined to assassinate their father Phraates; but the latter suggests, what has already been surmised, that it was as the avenger of his father that Orodes professed to take the field against Mithradates, while the title of $\epsilon\upsilon\pi\alpha\tau\omega\rho$ may very well have been taken by Mithradates from his namesake and contemporary the great ruler of Pontus (see Table III.). The second difference is of type. Mithradates always wears a jointed torquis with clasp in front, Orodes a spiral passing thrice round his neck. The portraits are very similar, as we might expect those of two brothers of not very different ages to be, but the lesser differences I have mentioned are sufficient to justify us in assuming two kings rather than one to have issued the series.

ARSACES XII. ORODES I.

(a). Early coinage.

Plate III. 15. *Obv.* Head of Orodes l. diad., neck-ornament spiral.
   Rev. ΒΑΞΙΛΕΩΞ ΒΑΞΙΛΕΩΝ ΜΕΓΑΛΟΥ ΑΡΞΑΚΟΥ ΚΑΙ ΚΤΙΞΤΟΥ. Arsaces seated r. on throne holding bow.
     Tetradrachm. Berlin.

16. *Obv.* As last.
   Rev. ΒΑΞΙΛΕΩΞ ΒΑΞΙΛΕΩΝ ΑΡΞΑΚΟΥ ΦΙΛΟΠΑΤΟΡΟΞ ΔΙΚΑΙΟΥ ΕΠΙΦΑΝΟΥΞ ΚΑΙ ΦΙΛΕΛΛΗΝΟΞ. Arsaces seated r.; to r. ⊠.
     Drachm. B.M. Wt. 57·7.

17. *Obv.* As last.
   Rev. Same inscr. without ΚΑΙ. Pegasus r. prancing; beneath, Ⱥ.
     B.M. Æ ·7.

18. *Obv.* Head of Orodes l., behind, Nike crowning him.
   Rev. Same inscr. Arsaces seated r.; to r. Ⱥ.
     Drachm. B.M. Wt. 60.

Plate III. 19.   *Obv.* As last.

         Rev. Same inscr. Eagle with spread wings standing r.; in front, 𝖠̅.

                               B.M. Æ ·6.

Varieties:—Of No. 16, monograms on rev ᚱ, K, etc. Of No. 17, types, horse's head r., bow case and club (B.M.). Of No. 18, monogram of rev. Ꙅᚱ (P.O.).

(β). Later coinage.

20.   *Obv.* Head of Orodes l. diademed, neck-ornament spiral.

     Rev. ΒΑΣΙΛΕΩΣ ΒΑΣΙΛΕΩΝ ΑΡΣΑΚΟΥ ΕΥΕΡΓΕΤΟΥ ΔΙΚΑΙΟΥ ΕΠΙΦΑΝΟΥΣ

       ΦΙΛΕΛΛΗΝΟΣ.   Arsaces seated r.; in front Ꙅᚱ.

               Drachm. B.M. Wt. 59·1.

21.   *Obv.* As last.

     Rev. Same inscr. Stag's head r.; on either side 𝖠, 𝖠̅.

                  B.M. Æ ·65.

22.   (*Obv.* As last.)

     Rev. Same inscr. Castle with four towers.

                  B.M. Æ ·55.

23.   *Obv.* Same head, behind, crescent (moon).

     (*Rev.* Same inscr. Arsaces seated r.; in front ⧖.)

               Drachm. B.M. Wt. 61·6.

24.   *Obv.* Same head between star and crescent (sun and moon).

     Rev. As last, mon. ᚱ.

               Drachm. B.M. Wt. 60·5.

25.   *Obv.* Head of Orodes l., on temple, wart, between star on one side, and star and crescent on
       the other.

     Rev. As last, mon. ᚱ, anchor in field.

               Drachm. B.M. Wt. 61.

26.   *Obv.* Similar to last, beard longer.

     Rev. As last, mon. 𝖠̅, anchor in field.

               Drachm. B.M. 56·7.

27.   *Obv.* Head of Orodes l. diad.; wart on temple.

     Rev. ΒΑΣΙΛΕΩΣ ΒΑΣΙΛΕΩΝ ΑΡΣΑΚΟΥ ΔΙΚΑΙΟΥ. Arsaces seated r.; in front 𝖠̅.

               Obol. B.M. Wt. 10.

28.   *Obv.* As last.

     Rev. ΒΑΣΙΛΕΩΣ ΒΑΣΙΛΕΩΝ ΑΡΣΑΚΟΥ ΟΡΩΔΟΥ. Same type, in front ᚱ.

               Obol. P.O.

Varieties:—Drachms of all the above types appear with a multitude of monograms. Types of copper, with obv. like Nos. 21–22, horse r., horse's head r., stag r.; with obv. like No. 23, horse r., Nike r.; with obv. like No. 24, bow in case, eagle r. holding wreath, horse's head r.; with obv. like No. 25, star, anchor and crescent, turreted head r., Nike r., helmeted head r., eagle r.; with obv. like No. 26, deer and eagle, turreted head r., eagle on amphora and grapes, ox head and ear of barley; with obv. like No. 27, crescent and star, palm and anchor, castle, eagle r. (all B.M.).

I have seen a diobol of this king, weight 17·4; obv., head of Orodes l., on forehead wart, in front palm; rev. that of obols twice struck.

ORODES I. AND PACORUS.

Plate III. 29.   *Obv.* Head of Orodes l. diad., without wart, between star and crescent.
   Rev. ΒΑΣΙΛΕΩΣ ΒΑΣΙΛΕΩΝ ΑΡΣΑΚΟΥ ΦΙΛΕΛΛΗΝΟΣ ΚΑΙ ΑΡΣΑΚΟΥ ΠΑΚΟ-
   ΡΟΥ.   Arsaces seated r.; behind, anchor, in front 𝕄.
   Drachm.   B.M.   Wt. 61·3.

   30.   As last, wart on forehead.
   Drachm.   B.M.   Wt. 61·6.

PACORUS I.

Plate IV. 1.   *Obv.* Head of Pacorus l. beardless, diad.; behind, Nike crowning it.
   Rev. ΒΑΣΙΛΕΩΣ ΒΑΣΙΛΕΩΝ ΑΡΣΑΚΟΥ ΕΥΕΡΓΕΤΟΥ ΔΙΚΑΙΟΥ ΕΠΙΦΑΝΟΥΣ
   ΦΙΛΕΛΛΗΝΟΣ.   Arsaces seated r.; behind, crescent, in front Ⱥ.
   Drachm.   B.M.   Wt. 58·1.

   2.   *Obv.* As last.
   Rev. Traces of same inscr.?   Head r. in pileus with short beard; in front Ⱥ.
   B.M.   Æ ·35.

Of the earlier coinage of Orodes I have already spoken, and shown how I divide it from the coins of his brother. The tetradrachm No. 15 belongs to a not uncommon class, which have been given in turn to several Kings. But the portrait is exactly the same on this coin as on the drachms and copper coins Nos. 16–19, even to the neck-ornament, which, as I have above remarked, is distinctive of Orodes. The title κτίστης suits Orodes better than any of the later Parthian Kings, for in his reign the Empire became consolidated, and put on a new footing; or, if the term be taken to mean only that the King founded a new city, who was more likely to do this than Orodes? Those tetradrachms which are usually given to Orodes I shall show, in speaking of the coins of Tiridates II., to belong, beyond doubt, to that monarch. After the middle of Orodes' reign the legend of the Parthian drachms varies but little. The number of mint-monograms increases largely in this reign, and a number of new ones come in, most of which do not again appear. They may have belonged to places in Asia Minor and Syria, both of which districts were overrun by the armies of Orodes. To Asia Minor and Syria, as I conjecture, belong in a special degree the coins which bear the name, as well as those which bear the portrait of Pacorus, who there took the title of King by his father's permission. The portrait on the drachm No. 1 seems to be certainly of Pacorus; as to the legend on Orodes' coins, I felt inclined to hesitate, as I have never seen a specimen with the word Πακόρου clear and unmistakable; but the reading has long been accepted, and I have no sufficient reason for calling it in doubt. It will be observed that the words καὶ Ἀρσάκου begin near the top of the coin behind the seated figure of the founder, and are continued under that figure. The second head on the copper coin No. 2 would seem to be that of some subordinate ruler or feudatory, but this is not certain.

The anchor which makes its appearance on some of these pieces is doubtless the representative of that anchor which the Seleucidæ adopted into their arms in consequence of a family legend, which also appears on the coins of Seleucus I. and Antiochus I., and which was adopted or copied by several of the princes of Central Asia, notably King Kamnaskires and his descendants. The wart, which appears on the forehead of Orodes, is imitated by many of his successors.

ARSACES XIII. PHRAATES IV.

Plate IV. 3. *Obv.* Head of Phraates l. diad., on forehead wart.
  Rev. ΒΑΣΙΛΕΩΣ ΒΑΣΙΛΕΩΝ ΑΡΣΑΚΟΥ ΕΥΕΡΓΕΤΟΥ ΔΙΚΑΙΟΥ ΕΠΙΦΑΝΟΥΣ ΦΙΛΕΛΛΗΝΟΣ. Date · · Ϛ ΥΓΕΡΒΕΡΕ. Phraates seated r., before him Pallas or Roma? armed holding wreath and spear.

  Tetradrachm. B.M. Wt. 227·7.

4. (*Obv.* As last.)
  Rev. Same inscr. Date — ΟΛΩΟΥ. Phraates seated r., before him City l. holding palm and cornucopiæ.

  Tetradrachm. B.M. Wt. 215·4.

5. *Obv.* As last.
  Rev. Same inscr. Date ΕΠΣ ΟΔΑΙΣΙ. Phraates seated l., holding Nike, who offers him wreath and sceptre.

  Tetradrachm. B.M. Wt. 231.

6. *Obv.* Same head, behind, eagle l., holding wreath in beak.
  Rev. Same inscr. Arsaces seated r., behind him eagle, holding in beak wreath; in front 𝕋.

  Drachm. B.M. Wt. 59·5.

7. *Obv.* Same head.
  Rev. Traces of same inscr.? Humped bull r.; above 𝕋.

  B.M. Æ ·45.

8. *Obv.* Same head, in front star; behind, eagle holding wreath in beak l.
  Rev. Same inscr. Arsaces seated r.; behind, star, in front 𝕋.

  Drachm. B.M. Wt. 58.

Plate IV. 9. *Obv.* As last.
    Rev. Same inscr. ? Male winged figure l.; in front ⍟.
        B.M. Æ ·45.

   10. *Obv.* As last.
     Rev. Same inscr. Sphinx, r.
         B.M. Æ ·35.

   11. *Obv.* Same head; in front star and crescent; behind, Nike with wreath l.
     Rev. Inscr. barbarous. Arsaces seated r.; behind, star, in front ⍟.
      Drachm. B.M. Wt. 59·4.

   12. *Obv.* Same head; in front star and crescent; behind, eagle holding wreath.
     Rev. Inscr. as Nos. 3–10. Arsaces seated r.; in front ⍟.
      Drachm. B.M. Wt. 56.

   13. *Obv.* As last.
     Rev. Date ΠϚ. Head of City r. wearing turreted crown.
        B.M. Æ ·55.

   14. *Obv.* As last.
     Rev. Inscr. as Nos. 3–10. Head of queen r. wearing tiara.
        B.M. Æ ·4.

   15. *Obv.* [As last.]
     Rev. Same inscr. ⍟.
        B.M. Æ ·45.

   16. *Obv.* [As last.]
     Rev. Same inscr. Æquitas l. holding scales; in field ⍟.
        B.M. Æ ·4.

   17. *Obv.* As last.
     Rev. Same inscr. ? Janiform male head.
        B.M. Æ ·45.

Varieties:—Of No. 6, monograms on rev. ⌐ᴾ, ✝, ⅄, and others (B.M.). Of No. 7, types of copper horse's head, ox-head, with two stars and crescent (B.M.). Of No. 8, monogram on rev. ⍟, ⅄ (B.M.) ⌐ᴾ (P.O.). Of Nos. 9–10 types of copper, fish r. (B.M.). Of No. 12, monogram on rev. ⍟ Δ (B.M.). Of Nos. 14–17 types of copper, horse r. and palm, Nike r., term and caduceus, winged male figure r., stag r., bunch of grapes between ears of barley, winged caduceus, Helios' head facing, two cornucopiæ, cantharus and star, Artemis Phosphoros, sea-horse, crescent and star (all B.M.). Of No. 13, on obv. head of King crowned by Nike, no star or crescent.

The dates of the tetradrachms in the British Museum begin with 285 Apellæus, and close

with 288 Xanthicus. Count von Prokesch-Osten begins with 281 Peritius. Visconti has
published a coin which bears the same head at an earlier stage, and the date 276 Gorpiæus.
Other coins are known as late as 289 Hyperberetæus. On the copper coins 280 is the only
date. It seems clear that all these coins were issued by the same King, and the dates prove
that this King was Phraates IV. At first sight the type which appears on the copper pieces,
such as No. 17, a Janus head, not unlike that on the coins of Rome, might have seemed
more appropriate to Tiridates, his contemporary and rival. And if the figure who on No. 3
presents a wreath to the King be held to represent Roma rather than Pallas, one might be
disposed here also to see an allusion to the part played by the Romans in putting forward
Tiridates. But a study of the dates of the tetradrachms which bear this type will soon show
that they must have been issued, not by Tiridates, but by Phraates. The date of the earliest
of these tetradrachms is, I believe, 284 Dæsius, and it was just about that period that, after
the flight of Tiridates, Phraates began to court the good-will of the ruler of Rome.

PHRAATES IV. or a usurper.

Plate IV. 18.   *Obv.* Head of a King l. diad.; on forehead, wart.
       Rev. ΒΑΣΙΛΕΩΣ ΒΑΣΙΛΕΩΝ ΑΡΣΑΚΟΥ ΕΥΕΡΓΕΤΟΥ ΑΥΤΟΚΡΑΤΩ (*sic*) ΕΠΙ-
       ΦΑΝΟΥΣ ΦΙΛΕΛΛΗΝΟΣ.   King seated r., before him a City l., holding palm and
       sceptre; date ΕΠΣ ΔΑΙ.
                    Tetradrachm.   B.M.   Wt. 181·3.

The date of this coin proves that it was minted during the reign of Phraates IV. The
head, however, is quite different from his, and closely resembles that on the coin (Pl. V. 1),
which is given to Orodes II. The title αὐτοκράτωρ also is not assumed by Phraates on his
certain coins. I am therefore obliged to leave this piece uncertain. History gives us no
information as to the events of the Seleucid year 285 (28/27 B.C.), when it was struck.

TIRIDATES II.

Plate IV. 19.   *Obv.* Head of Tiridates l. diad.; on forehead wart.
       Rev. ΒΑΣΙΛΕΩΣ ΒΑΣΙΛΕΩΝ ΑΡΣΑΚΟΥ ΕΥΕΡΓΕΤΟΥ ΔΙΚΑΙΟΥ ΕΠΙΦΑΝΟΥΣ
       ΦΙΛΕΛΛΗΝΟΣ.   Tiridates seated l., holding Nike and sceptre.
                    Tetradrachm.   B.M.   Wt. 231·6.

     20.   *Obv.* As last.
       Rev. Same inscr.   Tiridates seated r. on throne; before him City wearing mural crown,
       holding palm and sceptre; date ΔΥΣΤ.
                    Tetradrachm.   P.O.   Wt. 187·2.

     21.   *Obv.* As last.
       Rev. Same inscr.   Arsaces seated r.; in field Ⴔ ⅀Ɽ.
                    Drachm.   B.M.   Wt. 61·8.

On the tetradrachms of this class the only dates are in the year 280, the months Arte-misius, Dystrus and Dæsius (P.O.). They are usually given to Orodes in clear defiance of chronology, for we know that Orodes was dead in the year 280 (33/32 B.C.). But the year 33 B.C. was the exact time when Tiridates invaded Parthia, and compelled Phraates to fly to the Scyths. Nor is there at all an exact resemblance between the portrait of these tetra-drachms and that of the drachms of Orodes; the beard is shorter, and the aspect more truculent. The drachm (No. 21) bears a head closely similar to that of the tetradrachm, and the arrangement of the lines of the legend is not the same as in Orodes' coins. I have therefore removed it to this place, but without entire confidence.

ARSACES XIV. PHRAATACES.

Plate IV. 22. *Obv.* Head of Phraataces l. diad.; wart on forehead.
Rev. ΒΑΣΙΛΕΩΣ ΒΑΣΙΛΕΩΝ ΑΡΣΑΚΟΥ ΕΥΕΡΓΕΤΟΥ ΔΙΚΑΙΟΥ ΕΠΙΦΑΝΟΥΣ ΦΙΛΕΛΛΗΝΟΣ. Phraataces seated r., in front a city l., holding wreath and cornucopiæ. Date ΙΤ ΑΡΤΕΜΙΣΙ (?)
Tetradrachm. B.M. Wt. 226.

23. *Obv.* As last.
Rev. Same inscr. Arsaces I. seated r., holding bow. Date ΑΙΤ ΑΡΤΕΜΙΣΙ.
Tetradrachm. B.M. Wt. 208·4.

24. *Obv.* Head of Phraataces l.; on either side a wreath-bearing Nike.
Rev. Same inscr. Arsaces seated r.; in front Ⱥ.
Drachm. B.M. Wt. 54·4.

25. *Obv.* As last.
Rev. In place of inscription, circular border of dots. King r. on horseback; in front A.
B.M. Æ ·6.

26. *Obv.* As last.
Rev. Same border. Female figure l. holding palm, sacrificing at altar.
B.M. Æ ·55.

Varieties :—Of Nos. 25, 26, types of copper, crescent and star (B.M.), radiate head facing (P.O.).

PHRAATACES AND MUSA HIS MOTHER.

Plate IV. 27. *Obv.* ΒΑΣΙΛΕΩΣ ΒΑΣΙΛΕΩΝ. Head of Phraataces l. diad., in front Nike crowning it. Date ΔΙΤ.
Rev. ΘΕΑΣ ΟΥ —. Head of Musa r. wearing tiara; in front, Nike l. crowning it. Date ΟΛ (month Lous).
Tetradrachm. P.O. Wt. 211.

Plate IV. 28.   *Obv.* Head of Phraataces l. ; on either side a wreath-bearing Nike.
        Rev. ΘΕΑΣ ΟΥΡΑΝΙΑΣ ΜΟΥΣΗΣ ΒΑΣΙΛΙΣΣΗΣ.   Head of Musa l. in tiara; behind Ⱥ.
                  Drachm. B.M. Wt. 57·8.

Varieties :—Of No. 27, monogram on rev. 𝅘 (B.M.), Ⱥ and others. Copper coins with the same types (B.M.).

The dates on the coins of Phraataces and Musa known are 313 Xanthicus, 314 Lous, and 315 Hyperberetæus (all P.O.). The earliest known coin of Phraataces alone is No. 22, with the date 310 Artemisius ; the last would appear to be 313 Gorpiæus, published by Mionnet ; but this coin I have not seen.

In the reign of this King, the ordinary copper coins cease to bear a legend. A border of dots takes its place, or the type stands alone. Henceforward nearly all copper coins bear the monogram Ⱥ.

SANABARES OF BACTRIA.

Plate IV. 29.   *Obv.* Head of Sanabares l. in tiara; behind (L) ND (two Pehlvi letters.)
        Rev. ΒΑΣΙΛΕΥΣ ΜΕΓΑΣ ΣΑΝΑΒΑ.   Arsaces seated l; in front Ⱥ. Date ΓΙΤ.
                  Drachm. B.M. Wt. 58·5.

I place this coin among those of the Arsacidæ on account both of its type and monogram. Sanabares must have been a rival, and for the time a successful rival, of Phraataces. That he was a Bactrian king is known from certain copper coins which he issued (Thomas, Early Sassanian Inscriptions, p. 121) bearing Bactrian types and inscriptions.

ARSACES XV. ORODES II.

Plate V. 1.   *Obv.* Head of Orodes l. diad.
        Rev. ΒΑΣΙΛΕΩΣ ΒΑΣΙΛΕΩΝ ΑΡΣΑΚΟΥ ΕΥΕΡΓΕΤΟΥ ΔΙΚΑΙΟΥ ΕΠΙΦΑΝΟΥΣ ΦΙΛ-
        ΕΛΛΗΝΟΣ.   Orodes seated l., holding bow and sceptre; in field l. EM. Date ΖΙΤ (317).
            Tetradrachm. Berlin. Wt. 175·9.

The exact correspondence of date leaves no doubt that this probably unique coin belongs to Orodes II. the king mentioned by Josephus. The head is remarkably like that on Pl. IV. 18, but as the dates of both coins are certain, this must be a mere coincidence. The letters EM probably represent the intercalary month Embolimus.

ARSACES XVII. VONONES I.

Plate V. 2.   *Obv.* ΒΑΣΙΛΕΥΣ ΒΑΣΙΛΕΩΝ ΟΝΩΝΗΣ. Head of Vonones l. diad. (Traces of previous
        striking, ΒΑΣΙΛΕΩΝ, back of head of Phraataces, and date ΔΙΤ).
        Rev. ΒΑΣΙΛΕΩΣ ΒΑΣΙΛΕΩΝ ΑΡΣΑΚΟΥ ΕΥΕΡΓΕΤΟΥ ΔΙΚΑΙΟΥ ΕΠΙΦΑΝΟΥΣ ΦΙΛ-
        ΕΛΛΗΝΟΣ.   Nike l. holding wreath and palm. Date ΒΚΤ ΥΠΕ.
        (Traces of previous striking, ΘΕΑΣ ΟΥΡΑΝΙ—, back of head of Musa.)
            Tetradrachm. Berlin. Wt. 177·5.

Plate V. 3. As last, also restruck on coin of Phraataces and Musa.

Tetradrachm. B.M. Wt. 212.

4. *Obv.* ΒΑΞΙΛΕΥΞ ΟΝΩΝΗΞ. Head of Vonones l. diad.
    Rev. ΒΑΞΙΛΕΥΞ ΟΝΩΝΗΞ ΝΕΙΚΗΞΑΞ ΑΡΤΑΒΑΝΟΝ. Nike r., holding palm; in front 🅰.

Drachm. B.M. Wt. 58·3.

5. *Obv.* Same.
    Rev. Same inscr. 🅰.

B.M. Æ ·55.

Varieties:—Of No. 5, types of rev. Nike r. (B.M.), eagle r. (P.O.); monogram of rev. ⌐ᴿ (B.M.).

The date of these tetradrachms, besides that above given, is 320 (P.O.). It will be at once observed in how many respects Vonones departs from the traditional types and legends of the Arsacidæ. His Roman training indisposed him to abide in these matters by prescription. Up to his time no name, except those of Orodes and Pacorus, had appeared on the coin. The present prince not only records his name, but also the fact that he had won a victory over Artabanus. To this victory all his types allude. The legend of the tetradrachms is obscure, the reason of which is that they are usually or always restruck on pieces of Phraataces.

ARSACES XVIII. ARTABANUS III.

Plate V. 6. *Obv.* Head of Artabanus l. diad.
    Rev. ΒΑΞΙΛΕΩΞ ΒΑΞΙΛΕΩΝ ΕΥΕΡΓΕΤΟΥ ΑΡΞΑΚΟΥ. Artabanus seated l. receiving palm from female figure and wreath from kneeling male figure. Date —Δ (334) ΥΠΕΡΒΕ.

Tetradrachm. B.M. Wt. 218·4.

7. *Obv.* (As last).
    Rev. ΒΑΞΙΛΕΩΞ ΒΑΞΙΛΕΩΝ ΑΡΞΑΚΟΥ ΕΥΕΡΓΕΤΟΥ ΔΙΚΑΙΟΥ ΕΠΙΦΑΝΟΥΞ ΦΙΛΕΛΛΗΝΟΞ. Artabanus seated l., receiving palm from a City who holds cornucopiæ. Date ΒΚΤ.

Tetradrachm. P.O. Wt. 190·3.

8. *Obv.* Head of Artabanus, facing, diad.
    Rev. ΒΑΞΙΛΕΩΞ ΒΑΞΙΛΕΩΝ ΔΙΚΑΙΟΥ ΕΠΙΦΑΝΟΥΞ. Artabanus l. on horseback receiving palm from a City who holds sceptre, beneath horse Α∕. Date ΤΛΗ.

Tetradrachm. B.M. Wt. 200.

9. *Obv.* Head of Artabanus l. diad.
    Rev. ΒΑΞΙΛΕΩΞ ΒΑΞΙΛΕΩΝ ΑΡΞΑΚΟΥ ΕΥΕΡΓΕΤΟΥ ΔΙΚΑΙΟΥ ΕΠΙΦΑΝΟΥΞ ΦΙΛΕΛΛΗΝΟΞ. Arsaces seated r.; in front 🅰.

Drachm. B.M. Wt. 58·3.

10. *Obv.* As last.
    Rev. Female head r., in front 🅰.

B.M. Æ ·5.

Plate V. 11.   *Obv.* As last.

       Rev. Two-handled cup; in field l. $\overline{\mathcal{A}}$.

                    B.M.   Æ ·5.

Varieties:—Of No. 9, on rev. behind king Ω (P.O.).   Of Nos. 10–11, types of rev. male winged figure l., crescent and star, horse's head l. (all B.M.).

The earliest date is 322; there is also a tetradrachm dated 323 (P.O.): then there seems to be a gap; the later coins range from 334 Xanthicus (Paris) to 338.   The type of No. 8 is interesting, this being the first occasion on which a Parthian king appears on horseback. Under this king the legends of the drachms begin to become corrupt, and this process goes on so fast that in about a century they cease to be in any way intelligible.   It is by the degree of corruption in the legend, chiefly, that the later drachms are classed.

Arsaces XIX.   Vardanes I.

Plate V. 12.   *Obv.* Head of Vardanes l. diad.; on forehead wart.

       Rev. ΒΑΣΙΛΕΩΣ ΒΑΣΙΛΕΩΝ ΑΡΣΑΚΟΥ ΕΥΕΡΓΕΤΟΥ ΔΙΚΑΙΟΥ ΕΠΙΦΑΝΟΥΣ ΦΙΛΕΛΛΗΝΟΣ.   Vardanes, seated r., receives palm from City, who holds cornucopiæ. Date ΕΝΤ ΑΡΤΕΜΕΙΣΙΟΥ.

           Tetradrachm.   B.M.   Wt. 213·7.

13.   *Obv.* Similar head, no wart.

       Rev. Same inscr. (corrupt).   Arsaces seated r.; in front $\overline{\mathcal{A}}$.

           Drachm.   B.M.   Wt. 59.

14.   *Obv.* Similar head, behind ΔΝΤ.

       Rev. ΒΟΥΛΗ.   City seated r. on throne, holds cornucopiæ.

                B.M.   Æ ·65.

15.   Similar.   Date ΕΝΤ.

                B.M.   Æ ·45.

16.   *Obv.* Similar head.

       Rev. Nike r. holding wreath, square border of dots.

                B.M.   Æ ·45.

17.   *Obv.* As last.

       Rev. Eagle r. holding wreath and palm, same border.

                B.M.   Æ ·5.

Varieties:—Of Nos. 16–17, types of rev. Nike r., male figure l. holding cornucopiæ (B.M.), caduceus, altar (P.O.).

Von Prokesch-Osten publishes a tetradrachm of this prince of the date 351 Gorpiæus;

this coin appears in his plates, and there, instead of A, one seems to see △. It must, however, be added that Dr. Friedländer, of Berlin, agrees with the former reading. Otherwise the earliest coin known is of 353 Panemus, also published by von Prokesch-Osten. The earliest specimen in the B.M. has the date 354 Apellæus. The latest known specimen is of 356 Lous (P.O.). The copper coins bear only the dates above mentioned, 354, 355. I read BOYΛH on the obverse of these coins, which legend is about this period extremely common on Græco-Roman coins of all parts of Asia Minor. We have here a still further proof, if one were needed, that these dated copper coins are a civic issue by some Greek city, perhaps Seleucia on the Tigris.

ARSACES XX. GOTERZES.

Plate V. 18. *Obv.* Head of Goterzes l. diad.; behind Γ.
Rev. ΒΑΣΙΛΕΩΣ ΒΑΣΙΛΕΩΝ ΑΡΣΑΚΟΥ ΕΠΙΦΑΝΟΥΣ ΔΙΚΑΙΟΥ ΕΥΕΡΓΕΤΟΥ ΓΩΤΑΡΖΟΥ. Goterzes, seated r., receives wreath from City, who holds cornucopiæ. Date ΖΝΤ ΠΑΝΑ.

Tetradrachm. B.M. Wt. 194·3.

19. *Obv.* Same head.
Rev. ΒΑΣΙΛΕΩΣ ΒΑΣΙΛΕΩΝ ΑΡΣΑΚΟΥ ΕΥΕΡΓΕΤΟΥ ΔΙΚΑΙΟΥ ΕΠΙΦΑΝΟΥΣ ΦΙΛΕΛΛΗΝΟΣ. Same type; date ΑΞΤ.

Tetradrachm. B.M. Wt. 211·4.

20. *Obv.* Similar head.
Rev. Same inscr. Arsaces seated r.; in front Ⱥ·
Drachm. B.M. Wt. 55·8.

21. *Obv.* As last.
Rev. Head of Queen r., wearing tiara; round border of dots.
B.M. Æ ·6.

22. *Obv.* As last.
Rev. King l. sacrificing at altar, same border.
B.M. Æ ·5.

23. *Obv.* As last.
Rev. Upper part of Artemis r. holding bow and arrow, same border.
B.M. Æ ·5.

24. *Obv.* As last.
Rev. Male head l., slightly bearded, in tiara; same border.
B.M. Æ ·5.

25. *Obv.* As last.
Rev. ΓΩΤΕΡΖΗΣ ΒΑΣΙΛΕΥΣ ΒΑΣΙΛΕΩΝ ΥΟΣ ΚΕΚΑΛΟΥΜΕΝΟΣ ΑΡΤΑΒΑΝΟΥ. Arsaces seated r.; in front Ⱥ·
Drachm. Paris.

Plate V. 26. As last.

Drachm. St. Petersburgh.

Varieties:—Of No. 20, several barbarous imitations. Of Nos. 21–24, types of copper very numerous; among them, king seated holding bow or palm, male or female figure holding palm, Helios' head facing, thunderbolt, head of city r., armed female figure, horse r., King r. on horseback, horse's head r., fish, eagle l., amphora, wreath, pomegranate, cornucopiæ, caduceus, griffin's head, standard, trophy.

The earliest date is 352 (P.O.). This coin seems to be a memorial of the first reign of Goterzes, which lasted but a short time. The next is 356 Peritius (B.M.), from which date there is an uninterrupted series for every year until 362. The last coin is 362 Dæsius (B.M.), for the coin which is published by P.O. as 364 Dæsius must really bear the date 361, as Δ and Λ are not easily distinguishable, and Goterzes was certainly dead by the year 364.[1]

The drachms Nos. 25, 26, have long been known, but unfortunately no new specimen appears to confirm the reading. It is supposed that the mysterious words ΥΟΣ ΚΕΚΑΛΟΥΜΕΝΟΣ stand for υἱος κεκλημένος, and mean only that Goterzes claimed, and was proud of his descent from Artabanus. I regret that I have no better explanation to offer.

Arsaces XXI. Vonones II.
No coin.

Arsaces XXII. Vologeses I.

Plate V. 27. *Obv.* Head of Vologeses l. diad.; on forehead, wart.
Rev. ΒΑΣΙΛΕΩΣ ΒΑΣΙΛΕΩΝ ΑΡΣΑΚΟΥ ΕΥΕΡΓΕΤΟΥ ΔΙΚΑΙΟΥ ΕΠΙΦΑΝΟΥΣ ΦΙΛΕΛΛΗΝΟΣ. Vologeses, seated l., receives wreath from City who holds sceptre. Date ΓΞΤ.

Tetradrachm. B.M. Wt. 211·7.

28. *Obv.* As last.
Rev. Same inscr. Arsaces seated r.; in front Ⱥ.
Drachm. B.M. Wt. 55·9.

29. *Obv.* As last.
Rev. Horse's head r.; in front Ⱥ.
B.M. Æ ·45.

30. *Obv.* As last, behind (ول) ال (Vol).
Rev. As last but one.
Drachm. B.M. Wt. 53.

Varieties:—Of No. 29, types of copper, female figure between standards (B.M.), horseman r. (P.O.).

---

[1] Against this merely d *priori* statement of mine I must set Dr. Friedländer's opinion, that the date on the piece is really 364. He has obligingly sent me a cast, but I must confess that the date of the piece does not seem to me clear enough to overthrow the distinct statements of Tacitus.

The earliest date is 362 Gorpiæus (Paris); whence a continued series to 365 Hyperberetæus (P.O.).   Hence it will be seen that the entire reign of Vonones must have been comprised in the months of Panemus and Lous of the year 362.   This is quite consistent with the statements of Tacitus.   Some writers suppose the whole of the above coins to belong to Vonones, to whom they give a reign of five or six years.   To Vologeses they assign the coins of 367–9, which I give to Vardanes, as will appear below.   But it is put beyond any reasonable doubt, by the express statement of Tacitus, that Vologeses was King in 51 (362–3), and there is no clear evidence to the contrary.   On the drachm No. 30, we have for the first time (save in the case of Sanabares) Pehlvi letters, forming the beginning of the King's name.

VARDANES II.

Plate VI. 1.   *Obv.*   Head of Vardanes l. diad.; on forehead, wart.
         Rev. ΒΑΣΙΛΕΩΣ ΒΑΣΙΛΕΩΝ ΑΡΣΑΚΟΥ ΕΥΕΡΓΕΤΟΥ ΔΙΚΑΙΟΥ ΕΠΙΦΑΝΟΥΣ
         ΦΙΛΕΛΛΗΝΟΣ.   Vardanes seated l. receives wreath from City, who holds sceptre.
         Date ΖΞΤ.
                  Tetradrachm.   B.M.   Wt. 187.

     2.   *Obv.* As last.
         Rev.   BNANO
               ΔΙΟΣ
                       B.M.   Æ ·5.

     3.   *Obv.* Head of Vardanes facing in tiara, on either side, star.
         Rev. Inscr. as No. 1.   Arsaces seated r.; in front 𝕏.
             Drachm. B.M.   Wt. 56·3.

Varieties:—Copper of same obv. type as No. 3, on rev. male figure r. in niche holding eagle.

The date of the tetradrachms varies from 367 Apellæus (P.O.) to 369 Panemus (Paris). This period is just that assigned by Tacitus to the revolt of Vardanes.   The head of the King is quite youthful.   The legend of No. 2 is very curious, and must remain doubtful until another specimen appears.   A very slight liberty taken with the letters as they appear would transform them into BAPANO, the very name of Bardanes; but it is to be observed that the Parthians did not usually thus run the letters of a name together, a practice of which one could find a hundred instances in the contemporary Greek-Imperial coinage of Asia Minor.

VOLOGESES II.

Plate VI. 4.   *Obv.* Head of Vologeses l. diad.
         Rev. ΒΑΣΙΛΕΩΣ ΒΑΣΙΛΕΩΝ ΑΡΣΑΚΟΥ ΕΥΕΡΓΕΤΟΥ ΔΙΚΑΙΟΥ ΕΠΙΦΑΝΟΥΣ
         ΦΙΛΕΛΛΗΝΟΣ.   Vologeses seated l., receives palm from City turreted: date ΔΠΤ
         ΞΑΝΔΙΚ.
             Tetradrachm. B.M.   Wt. 224·4

Plate VI. 5. *Obv.* As last.

  Rev. Same inscr. Arsaces seated r. ; in front $\overline{\overline{\mathcal{A}}}$.

    Drachm. B.M. Wt. 57·8.

  6. *Obv.* As last.

  Rev. Caduceus winged; square border of dots.

    B.M. Æ ·6.

Varieties:—Of No. 6; types of copper, King sacrificing (in field l. crescent), Pallas? facing holding shield and spear, altar, crux ansata, horse's head (B.M.), eagle with wreath (P.O.).

The dates of the tetradrachms from 372 (P.O.) and 374 Xanthicus (B.M.) to 379 (P.O.).

Count von Prokesch-Osten publishes these coins as of Artabanus IV., to whom also he gives the piece, of quite another character, described below with the date 392. The reason of this attribution is obscure, for it is quite clear, from the notices of the historians, that *a* Vologeses was reigning in Parthia at this time, and no name appears on the coins themselves. In none of the writers is there any indication that the Vologeses of 372–9 is a different King from the Vologeses of 351. If we had no coins, we should assume that the old King put down the rebellion of his son, and continued to reign. But it is at least a curious fact, that the portrait and style of the later coins which follow those of Vardanes, is quite different from the portrait and style of the earlier coins which precede them. One of two things seems to have happened. Either, after overthrowing his son, the old Vologeses began the issue of a reformed coinage, adorned with a more recent portrait of himself. Or else the elder monarch did not survive the defeat of his son, and dying, left his power to another son bearing his own name. The latter alternative is somewhat more probable numismatically, the former historically, and it is most rational to refuse finally to decide between them until more evidence shall be discovered.

PACORUS II.

(a). Wearing diadema.

Plate VI. 7. *Obv.* Young head of Pacorus l. diad.; behind B.

  Rev. ΒΑΣΙΛΕΩΣ ΒΑΣΙΛΕΩΝ ΑΡΣΑΚΟΥ ΠΑΚΟΡΟΥ ΔΙΚΑΙΟΥ ΕΠΙΦΑΝΟΥΣ ΦΙΛΕΛΛΗΝΟΣ. Pacorus seated l., receives wreath from turreted City r. who holds sceptre. Date ΘΠΤ.

    Tetradrachm. B.M. Wt. 218.

  8. *Obv.* (Same head; behind Γ.)

  Rev. Same inscr. Pacorus l. on horseback receives wreath from City who holds sceptre; behind her, warrior r. Date ΒϘΤ ΔΥΣΤ?

    Tetradrachm. B.M. Wt. 204.

  9. *Obv.* Same head. Date ΔϘΤ.

  Rev. Head of City r. turreted.

    B.M. Æ ·55.

Plate VI. 10. *Obv.* Same head.
   Rev. Usual inscr. debased. Arsaces seated r.; in front 𝔸.
     Drachm. B.M. Wt. 57·9.

 11. *Obv.* Same head.
   Rev. Vase.

     B.M. Æ ·45.

Varieties:—Of No. 11, rev. YEΔCAC bird r. Of Nos. 7, 8, letters behind head A, B, Γ, Δ.

    (β). Wearing helmet.

 12. *Obv.* Head of Pacorus l. slightly bearded, in helmet; behind, B.
   Rev. Inscr. and type as No. 7. Date ΔY ΓΟΡΠΙΑΙ.
     Tetradrachm. Berlin. Wt. 143·1.

 13. *Obv.* Same head.
   Rev. As No. 10.
     Drachm. B.M. Wt. 53·7.

 14. *Obv.* Same head.
   Rev. Head of City r. Date CY.
     B.M. Æ ·45.

Varieties:—Copper, obv. as No. 13, rev. wild goat l. (P.O.), Nike r. (B.M.).

The dates of the tetradrachms are 389 Dæsius (Paris) to 393 (B.M.) and 394 (P.O.) for the beardless and diademed head. For the bearded head, nearly always in helmet, the dates are 404 Panemus (P.O.) and 404 (Bank of England) to 407 Dystrus (P.O.). There are also copper coins of 391, 394, 395 (B.M.), 406 (Bank of England).

The coins of Pacorus bring us to an important innovation, the name of the King at full-length on the tetradrachms. And the reason of this change is clear, for we find at this time no less than three Kings, Pacorus, Artabanus, and Vologeses, reigning simultaneously. The name was therefore necessary to prevent the portraits and coinages of the Kings from becoming confused. Of the smaller coins one of the most remarkable is the small copper piece with the legend YEΔξAξ, as to the meaning of which word I am in entire ignorance. There seems to be a break in the reign of Pacorus from A.S. 395 to 404. When, after this break, coins again appèar, they represent the King as bearded; before, he was beardless.

ARTABANUS IV.

Plate VI. 15. *Obv.* Head of Artabanus l. diad.
   Rev. ΒΑξΙΛΕΩξ ΒΑξΙΛΕΩΝ ΑΡξΑΚΟY ΑΡΤΑΒΑΝΟY ΔΙΚΑΙΟY ΕΠΙΦΑΝΟYξ ΦΙΛΕΛΛΗΝΟξ. Artabanus seated l. receives untied diadem from City; date BϘT.
     Tetradrachm. B.M. Wt. 203·6.

Another piece in the B.M. has the date 392 Panemus. Coins with the same date (the month not legible) exist also at Paris and Berlin. I am not aware of any coin existing with the name of Artabanus and another date. This King must have been a contemporary of Pacorus; I have mentioned above (p. 14) the facts known in connexion with him. Other coins which may have been issued by him will be found at the bottom of Plate VI.

CHOSROES.

Plate VI. 16. *Obv.* Head of Chosroes l. diad.
     Rev. Head of City r. Date HIY.

          B.M. Æ ·45.

17. *Obv.* Same head, great tufts of hair.
     Rev. Same type. Date HKY.

          B.M. Æ ·85.

18. *Obv.* Same head, full face.
     Rev. Same type. Date ΘKY.

          B.M. Æ ·45.

19. *Obv.* Same head l. in crown with three points.
     Rev. Head of City r. her hand visible holding wreath. Date BΛY.

          B.M. Æ ·45.

20. *Obv.* Same head l. in helmet with cheek-pieces.
     Rev. City r., holding palm bound with fillet. Date ΘΛY.

          B.M. Æ ·75.

21. *Obv.* As No. 17.
     Rev. Usual inscr. debased. Arsaces seated r.; in front Ⓐ.

          Drachm. B.M. Wt. 54·7.

Varieties of No. 20, type of rev. City seated l., same date.

These coins are connected together by the general similarity of the portrait throughout. The most salient feature of that portrait is the great tufts of hair, probably artificial, on both sides of the head, which are found on all coins, except those with the dates 418–19, which two pieces may belong to another of the many rivals, who at this time contested among themselves the succession to the throne of the Arsacidæ. The dates of the copper pieces, besides those given above, are 419, 421, 424, 431 (B.M.), 423, 430 (P.O.), 426, 427, 437. As these dates fall into the period during which we know Chosroes to have reigned, we naturally give him the coins. His desperate wars with Trajan may furnish us with an explanation of the rarity of his silver coins, and the total absence of tetradrachms. It is certain that many tetradrachms were issued by a Vologeses during the latter part of this reign; but unfortunately history does not furnish us with the means of deciding which part of the Parthian dominions belonged to each competitor.

MITHRADATES IV.

Plate VI. 22.   *Obv.* Head of Mithradates l. diad.

   Rev. (מתרדת מלכא) מתרדת מלכא (Matradat Malka),[1] and barbarized Greek inscr.   Arsaces seated r., in front 𝔸.

     Drachm.   B.M.   Wt. 54·4.

  23.   *Obv.* Same head.

   Rev. Head of Herakles or a Satrap r. bare; behind I; above ΔK (year 424?).

    East India House.   Æ ·5.

It is a great pity that this last coin, which should be invaluable for fixing the date of Mithradates, should be in poor condition.   ΔK appear to be certain, and there is space for another letter, which can scarcely have been any but Y, for the style of the drachms fixes them to the period between Pacorus II. and Vologeses III.   On the other hand, the I is distinct, and it is quite uncertain what it may mean.   The aspect of the coin is not that of the ordinary Parthian pieces; it may have been issued by a satrap, if Mithradates, himself unknown to history, can be supposed to have had satraps under him.

ARTABANUS IV. OR MITHRADATES IV.

Plate VI. 24.   *Obv.* Head of a King l. diad.

   Rev. Inscr. corrupt.   Arsaces seated r.; in front 𝔸.

    Drachm.   B.M.   Wt. 54·4.

  25.   Similar.

    Drachm.   B.M.   Wt. 55·8.

  26.   Similar.

    Drachm.   B.M.   Wt. 55·7.

  27.   *Obv.* Similar head.

   Rev. Eagle r.

     B.M.   Æ ·5.

  28.   *Obv.* Similar head.

   Rev. Humped bull reclining r.; above, crescent.

     B.M.   Æ ·45.

Varieties of Nos. 27–28, types of copper, bull's head facing, cow's head l., dolphin r., griffin r. (B.M.), emblem ♎, Arsaces seated (P.O.).

The above are a few varieties of the many Parthian drachms and copper coins of rude

---

[1] For this and the following transcriptions of Pehlvi legends, the Editor has kindly made himself responsible.

workmanship and debased legend which abound. That they are later than Pacorus II. appears from a comparison of legends, and, on the other hand, they appear to precede the pieces of the Vologeses III.–VI., because the head on them is diademed; while the head of the later princes always wears a helmet. They therefore fall into the reigns of Artabanus IV., Mithradates IV., and their contemporaries.

VOLOGESES III.

Plate VII. 1. *Obv.* Head of Vologeses l. wearing helmet, around the edge of which are what look like hooks; behind △.

   Rev. ΒΑΣΙΛΕΩΣ ΒΑΣΙΛΕΩΝ ΑΡΣΑΚΟΥ ΟΛΑΓΑΣΟΥ ΔΙΚΑΙΟΥ ΕΠΙΦΑΝΟΥΣ ΦΙΛΕΛΛΗΝΟΣ. Vologeses, seated l., receives wreath from a City who holds sceptre. Date ϙ Τ.

      Tetradrachm. B.M. Wt. 212·6.

  2. *Obv.* Same head, behind, Ε.

   Rev. As last. Date ΓΛΥ ΠΕΡΙΤΕΙΟΥ.

      Tetradrachm. B.M. Wt. 206·8.

  3. *Obv.* Same head.

   Rev. Head of City r. turreted and veiled. Date ΗΛΥ.

      B.M. Æ ·65.

  4.[1] *Obv.* Head facing in helmet with cheek-pieces. Date ΘΛΥ.

   Rev. City seated l., hand raised to head; in front, palm.

      B.M. Æ ·7.

  5. *Obv.* Head as No. 1.

   Rev. Inscr. corrupt. Arsaces seated r.; in front 𝔸.

      Drachm. B.M. Wt. 54·6.

  6. *Obv.* Same head; behind ⅃ꠤ (Vol).

   Rev. (As last.)

  7. *Obv.* Same head.

   Rev. Eagle l. in wreath, beak.

      B.M. Æ ·5.

Varieties of Nos. 1–2; on obv. Α, Β, Γ.

The dates of the tetradrachms are as follows: 389 (B.M.), 389 Dæsius (P.O.), 390 (B.M.), 390 Dæsius (P.O.), 390 Embolimus (the intercalary month, the Marquis de Lagoy, Rev. Num. 1855); then a break, after which a constant succession from 431 (B.M.) to 449 Dius (B.M.), and 450 Apellæus (P.O.). The other dates of the copper are 423, 424, 430, 438, 439 (B.M.), 434,

---

[1] I am not sure that this piece might not with almost as great propriety be given to Chosroes.

435, 437 (P.O.). Count de Salis has left a note of a tetradrachm bearing the date 460, but without stating where he saw it. We here reach a well-known *crux* of Parthian numismatics. We have two series of coins, of which one covers the years 389–90, the other the years 423–450 (or even 460). The head on all these coins is unmistakably the same, but style and metal both become ruder as years go on (*cf.* No. 1 with No. 2). It seems impossible to avoid the conclusion that both series belong to the same King, and that the name of that King was Vologeses we know from the legend. The historians inform us of a Vologeses who was reigning about the year 442 (130 A.D.), and it is clearly this prince who issued our coins. During the earlier part of his rule, which corresponds with the reign of Pacorus, he can have possessed but a small part of Parthia, and the Roman historians, who give us an account of the war of Trajan and Chosroes, never once mention his name. And in fact the cessation of his coinage during that war seems to point to his temporary effacement. On the death of Chosroes, he seems to have become sole Parthian king. We have fair numismatic evidence, then, for a reign of 61 years by this prince, a thing which is the more remarkable, as the head on his very earliest pieces is that of a bearded man, who must apparently be at least twenty-five years of age.

VOLOGESES IV.

Plate VII. 8. *Obv.* Head of Vologeses l. in helmet with back-piece; behind B.

Rev. ΒΑΣΙΛΕΩΣ ΒΑΣΙΛΕΩΝ ΑΡΣΑΚΟΥ ΟΛΑΓΑΣΟΥ ΔΙΚΑΙΟΥ ΕΠΙΦΑΝΟΥΣ ΦΙΛ-ΕΛΛΗΝΟΣ. Vologeses, seated l., receives wreath from City who holds sceptre. Date ΔΞΥ ΑΠΕΛΛΑΙΟΥ.

Tetradrachm. B.M. Wt. 208·8.

9. *Obv.* Same head. Date ΕΟΥ.
Rev. Head of City r.; in front A.

B.M. Æ ·6.

10. *Obv.* Head l. in helmet with cheek-pieces.
Rev. (ولگشي ملکا) ולגשי מלכא (Volgasi Malka). Greek inscr. illegible. Arsaces seated r.; in front Ⱥ.

Drachm. B.M. Wt. 55.

11. *Obv.* Same head.
Rev. City seated r.; holds palm and cornucopiæ.

B.M. Æ ·35.

12. *Obv.* As No. 8.
Rev. (ولگشي ارشك ملکين ملکا) ולגשי ארשך מלכין מלכא (Volgasi Arsak Malkin Malka). Religious symbol.

B.M. Æ ·85.

Varieties of No. 11, type of rev. ✕.

The tetradrachms are extremely numerous; their dates vary from 460 Dius (B.M.) to 502 (P.O. and Paris). The copper coins from 460 (P.O.) to 488 (B.M.). The head on the drachms differs somewhat from that on the larger coins, but not enough to throw any doubt on their representing the same personage.   No. 12 is a piece the legend of which was first read by Mr. Thomas (Num. Chron. vol. xii.).   It was doubtless struck in the south of Parthia, and the characters it bears are of the class called by Mr. Thomas Persepolitan Pehlvi. The meaning of the type, a common one on Parthian coins, is obscure, but it is possible it may represent the sun, the great object of Zoroastrian worship.

The difference of the portrait on the above pieces from that on the tetradrachms of years 431–450 is so great as to render it certain that at this point a new King succeeded.   That his name was Vologeses we learn from the historians.

VOLOGESES V.

Plate VII. 13.   *Obv.* Head of Vologeses, facing, with tufts of hair on either side; to r. **A**.
    Rev. Traces of same legend as last King.   Vologeses, seated l., receives wreath from City,
     who holds sceptre.   Date BΦ ΓΟΡΠ.

         Tetradrachm.   B.M.   Wt. 195·4.

   14.   *Obv.* Same head l.
    Rev. Similar.   Date ΔΦ.

         Tetradrachm.   B.M.   Wt. 197·6.

   15.   *Obv.* Head as No. 13.
    Rev. (ولگشی ملکا) ולגשי מלכא (Volgasi Malka) and corrupt Greek legend.   Arsaces
     seated r.; in front Ⱥ.
         Drachm.   Hunter Mus.

   16.   *Obv.* As last.
    Rev. Eagle l. wings spread.
         B.M.   Æ ·5.

Varieties of No. 16. type of rev. fore-part of Pegasus r. (P.O.), Griffin r. (B.M.).

The dates begin with 502 Gorpiæus (B.M.) and continue to 514 Audinæus (B.M.), 519 (Bank of England), 520 (cabinet Magnoncour).

VOLOGESES VI.

Plate VII. 17.   *Obv.* Head of Vologeses l. in helmet with back-piece; behind B.
    Rev. Traces of inscr. and type as No. 13.   Date AKΦ.
        Tetradrachm.   B.M.   Wt. 201·7.

   18.   *Obv.* Similar head ; behind ול (Vol).
    Rev. (ولگشی ملکا) ולגשי מלכא (Volgasi Malka) and corrupt Greek legend.   Arsaces
     seated r.; in front Ⱥ.
        Drachm.   B.M.   Wt. 58·6.

Varieties of No. 18 :—there are also copper coins with, as type, eagle bearing wreath (B.M.).

The dates of the tetradrachms begin with 520 (P.O.) and 521 (B.M.), and continue to 533 (B.M.) There is at Paris a coin with very similar type and corrupt legend, bearing the date 539. This piece is interesting, as we know that Artabanus was defeated and slain by the Persians before A.S. 539. We may therefore, with some confidence, conclude that Vologeses, about whom history, curiously enough, tells us nothing, lived and reigned a year longer than his brother. Or it is possible that the coin may have been issued by Artavasdes (see below). I have seen the piece, and it appears to me that the portrait does not materially differ from that on coins of earlier date.

ARTABANUS V.

Plate VII. 19. *Obv.* Head of Artabanus l. in helmet with cheek-pieces.

    Rev. הרתבי מלכא (هرتي ملكا) (Hartabi Malka) and corrupt Greek legend. Arsaces seated r. ; in front 𝔸.

        Drachm. B.M. Wt. 56·4.

Varieties : copper with types of rev. wild-goat l. (B.M.), eagle l. (P.O.).

It is not a little singular that of the two brothers, Vologeses and Artabanus, the latter should consistently be mentioned as King by the Roman historians at the time of Caracalla's invasion, yet that the former should apparently have issued all the tetradrachms. For I believe that wherever a tetradrachm of this period bears any legible name, it is always that of Vologeses.

ARTAVASDES.

Plate VII. 20. *Obv.* Head of Artavasdes l. in helmet with cheek-pieces, beard forked ; behind >V=אר.

    Rev. ארתבזו מלכא (ارتبزو ملكا) (Artabazu Malka) and corrupt Greek legend. Arsaces seated r. ; in front 𝔸.

        Drachm. B.M. Wt. 56.

Varieties : type of copper, rev. eagle l. holding wreath (P.O.).

This coin gives us the name of the successor of Artabanus, who strove vainly after his death to resist the growing power of the Persians, and soon fell, dragging with him the whole Parthian Empire.

DATED CIVIC COINS.

Plate VII. 21. *Obv.* Head of City r. wearing turreted crown.

    Rev. SKT VΠEPBEPETAIOY. Veiled female head r. ; behind ✕.

        P.O. Æ ·5.

22. *Obv.* Head of City r. wearing turreted crown.

    Rev. ΠΟΛΙΣ A . City seated l. on rocks, holding in r. Nike ; beneath her issues l. a horned river-god.

        B.M. Æ ·3.

23. *Obv.* As last.

    Rev. ΔΚΣ
        ΔΙΟΥ
        A

        B.M. Æ ·3.

Plate VII. 24.   *Obv.* As last.

> *Rev.* BNT. Nike l. holding palm.

B.M. Æ ·3.

Varieties :—Of No. 21, date 327 Hyperb. (Imhoof-Blumer). Of No. 24, date 353 (B.M.). The city of Seleucia ad Tigrim also issued coins dated 270 (B.M.).

The date A.S. 326 Hyperberetæus of coin No. 21 falls within the reign of Artabanus III. As at this time Artabanus was occupied in an expedition into Armenia, where he set up his son Orodes as governor, Von Prokesch-Osten thinks that this coin is a memorial of the brief reign of the latter prince. In the monogram he reads, by what method I know not, the name of Artaxata, capital of Armenia. The attribution to Orodes is possible, but by no means established ; but the place of mintage quite uncertain.

No. 22 is not dated, but is very interesting as giving a proof that the monogram **A** or **Ā** stands for a city. This city stood on a river, but we can ascertain nothing more about it.

No. 23. The date 1st of Dius of the year 324, that is to say, the 1st day of the 324th year of the Seleucidæ, unfortunately falls into a period of history which is to us quite blank. Some great event must have on that day taken place. There is no sufficient reason for giving those pieces to Seleucia, as is usually done.

No. 24. This coin is probably a memorial of the revolt of Seleucia, which took place in the year A.D. 40. The city retained its freedom for seven years, and was then reduced by Vardanes.

Previously, in the reign of Orodes also, Seleucia had revolted, and was reduced, as we are told, by the Surenas. But as this revolt seems to have taken place before B.C. 54, the coin of Seleucia, dated 270, can scarcely have been issued during the brief period of autonomy.

APPENDIX.

Plate VII. 25.   *Obv.* Head of a king r. diad. ; behind $\underset{A}{\epsilon}$; border of dots and beads.

> *Rev.* ΒΑΣΙΛΕΩΣ ΚΑΜΝΑΣΚΙΡΟΥ ΝΙΚΗΦΟΡΟΥ.   Apollo seated l. on omphalos, holding arrow and bow ; border of dots.

Tetradrachm. Paris.

26.   *Obv.* Heads of a King and Queen l. ; behind, Seleucid anchor.

> *Rev.* ΒΑΣΙΛΕΩΣ ΚΑΜΝΑΣΚΙΡΟΥ ΚΑΙ ΒΑΣΙΛΙΣΣΗΣ ΑΝΖΑΖΗΣ. Zeus seated l. holding Nike and sceptre ; in ex. date ΑΛΣ.

Tetradrachm. B.M. Wt. 242.

The King Mnaskires has been so long one of the recognized rulers of Parthia, that I add the above two coins to my plate in order to justify me in excluding him. I have already observed (*suprà*, page 7), that all that Lucian testifies to is the existence of a Kamnaskires, who was Παρθυαίων βασιλεύς. But as Lucian places him not by the side of Sinatroces, among the true Parthian Kings, but among the rulers of Characene, it is probable that he was not an Arsacid, but a subordinate prince of some part of the Parthian dominions. This supposition is raised to the rank of a certainty by the evidence of the tetradrachms Nos. 25, 26. It is possible that these may have been issued by the same King, one in his youth, the other in his old age, but it is more probable that they were minted by different princes. Of No. 25, the type, the inscription, and the border all indicate the period of the Kings Antiochus IV.–V. of Syria, and Mithradates I. of Parthia. As to its place of issue, we have no clue.

No. 26 is supposed to have been struck in Susiana, chiefly because the piece is usually brought from that region. It seems to bear the date 231 ; and if this date be by the Seleucid era, the coin will have been issued in the year B.C. 82–1 ; a date by no means impossible, although we should have been inclined to prefer an earlier one.

There can be little doubt that one or other of these pieces was issued by the prince whom Lucian mentions.

P.S. It is probable, considering the extent of numismatic literature, that in many cases published coins have been omitted or overlooked in the preceding monograph. I have certainly overlooked a very important tetradrachm, published by Dr. von Sallet in the first volume of the Zeitschrift für Numismatik, plate viii. 3, p. 307.

Obv. Head of a Parthian King r. diademed; border of reels and beads.

Rev. ΒΑΣΙΛΕΩΣ ΑΡΣΑΚΟΥ. Demeter seated l. on throne supported by winged female monster; in her r. she holds Nike, who places a wreath on her head; in her l. cornucopiæ; in ex. two monograms 太 𝍏. *Tetradrachm.* Berlin. Wt. 225·3.

The head on the obverse of this piece is not exactly like that on the Parthian tetradrachms of Mithradates I., nor yet exactly like that on his coins of Greek work. But there is a general likeness to both; and there can be small doubt that the head is meant for Mithradates. The reverse-type is taken from the coins of Demetrius I., King of Syria, who reigned B.C. 162–150, a period which falls well into the reign of Mithradates.

TABLE I.

TABLE OF EARLIEST AND LATEST DATES ON COINS OF PARTHIAN KINGS.

KING.	EARLIEST A.S.	COLLECTION.	LATEST A.S.	COLLECTION.	REMARKS.
Phraapates	125	B.M.			Also in Berlin.
Mithradates I.	173	,,	174	B.M.	Issued by a Satrap.
Himerus	189	P.O.			Reign of Mithradates II.
Phraates IV.	276 Gor.	Munich	289 Hyp.	Paris	302 Hyp. in Subhi Bey's Catalogue.
Tiridates II.	280 Dys.	P.O.	280 Dæ.	P.O.	Usually given to Orodes.
Phraataces	310 Gor.	B.M.	313 Gor.	Magnoncour	
Phraataces and Musa	313 Xan.	P.O.	315 Hyp.	P.O.	
Orodes II.	317 Emb.	,,			
Vonones	320	,,	322 Hyp.	B.M.	
Artabanus III. 1st reign	322	,,	323	P.O.	
,, 2nd reign	334 Xan.	Mionnet	338	B.M.	
Vardanes I.	353 Pan.	P.O.	356 Lo.	P.O.	351 Gor. in P.O. is perhaps 354 Gor.
Goterzes 1st reign	352	,,			
,, 2nd reign	356 Per.	B.M.	362 Dæ.	B.M.	364 Dæ. in P.O. may be a mistake of the die-sinker for 361 Dæ.
Vonones II.					No coin known.
Vologeses I.	362 Gor.	Paris	365 Hyp.	P.O.	
Vardanes II.	367 Ape.	P.O.	369 Pan.	Paris	
Vologeses II.	374 Xan.	B.M.	379 Xan.	Magnoncour	372 P.O. This date is very doubtful.
Pacorus II. 1st reign	389 Dæ.	Paris	395	B.M.	
,, 2nd reign	404 Pan.	P.O.	407 Dys.	P.O.	
Artabanus IV.	392 Pan.	B.M.			
Chosroes	418	,,	439	B.M.	
Vologeses III. 1st reign	389 Dæ.	P.O.	390 Emb.	Lagoy	
,, 2nd reign	431	B.M.	450 Ape.	P.O.	460 published by Vaillant
Mithradates IV.	424	E.I.H.			
Vologeses IV.	460 Di.	B.M.	502	P.O.	
Vologeses V.	502 Gor.	,,	520	Magnoncour	
Vologeses VI.	520	P.O.	539	Paris	The Paris coin may be of Artavasdes.

⁎ B.M. is British Museum; P.O. Cabinet of Count von Prokesch-Osten; E.I.H. East India House.

TABLE II.

LIST OF TITLES ADOPTED BY PARTHIAN KINGS.

Arsaces I.	ΑΡΣΑΚΗΣ						
	ΒΑΣΙΛΕΥΣ ΑΡΣΑΚΗΣ						
Tiridates I.	ΒΑΣΙΛΕΥΣ ΜΕΓΑΣ ΑΡΣΑΚΗΣ						
Artabanus I.	"	"	"				
Phraapates	"	"	"				
	"	"	"	ΦΙΛΑΔΕΛΦΟΣ			
	"	"	"	"	ΦΙΛΕΛΛΗΝ		
Phraates I.	ΒΑΣΙΛΕΥΣ ΑΡΣΑΚΗΣ						
	ΒΑΣΙΛΕΥΣ ΜΕΓΑΣ ΑΡΣΑΚΗΣ						
	"	"	"	ΘΕΟΠΑΤΩΡ			
Mithradates I.	"	"	"				
	"	"	"	ΕΠΙΦΑΝΗΣ			
	"	"	"	ΦΙΛΕΛΛΗΝ			
	ΒΑΣΙΛΕΥΣ ΒΑΣΙΛΕΩΝ ΜΕΓΑΣ ΑΡΣΑΚΗΣ ΕΠΙΦΑΝΗΣ						
	"	"	ΑΡΣΑΚΗΣ ΕΥΕΡΓΕΤΗΣ ΔΙΚΑΙΟΣ ΚΑΙ ΦΙΛΕΛΛΗΝ				
Phraates II.	ΒΑΣΙΛΕΥΣ ΜΕΓΑΣ ΑΡΣΑΚΗΣ ΘΕΟΠΑΤΩΡ ΕΥΕΡΓΕΤΗΣ						
	"	"	"	"	"	ΕΠΙΦΑΝΗΣ ΦΙΛΕΛΛΗΝ	
Artabanus II.	"	"	"	"	ΝΙΚΑΤΩΡ		
Himerus	"	"	"	ΝΙΚΗΦΟΡΟΣ			
Mithradates II.	"	"	"	ΕΥΕΡΓΕΤΗΣ ΕΠΙΦΑΝΗΣ ΦΙΛΕΛΛΗΝ			
	"	"	"	"	"	ΚΑΙ ΦΙΛΕΛΛΗΝ	
	"	"	"	ΘΕΟΣ ΕΥΕΡΓΕΤΗΣ ΕΠΙΦΑΝΗΣ ΦΙΛΕΛΛΗΝ			
Sinatroces	"	"	"	ΑΥΤΟΚΡΑΤΩΡ ΦΙΛΟΠΑΤΩΡ ΕΠΙΦΑΝΗΣ ΦΙΛΕΛΛΗΝ			
Phraates III.	"	"	"	ΘΕΟΠΑΤΩΡ ΕΥΕΡΓΕΤΗΣ ΕΠΙΦΑΝΗΣ ΦΙΛΕΛΛΗΝ			
	"	"	"	"	"	"	ΚΑΙ ΦΙΛΕΛΛΗΝ
	"	"	"	ΦΙΛΟΠΑΤΩΡ ΕΥΕΡΓΕΤΗΣ ΕΠΙΦΑΝΗΣ ΦΙΛΕΛΛΗΝ			
Mithradates III.	"	"	"	ΕΠΙΦΑΝΗΣ ΔΙΚΑΙΟΣ ΘΕΟΣ ΕΥΠΑΤΩΡ ΦΙΛΕΛΛΗΝ			
	"	"	"	"	"	"	" ΚΑΙ ΦΙΛΕΛΛΗΝ
	ΒΑΣΙΛΕΥΣ ΒΑΣΙΛΕΩΝ ΜΕΓΑΣ ΑΡΣΑΚΗΣ ΔΙΚΑΙΟΣ ΕΠΙΦΑΝΗΣ ΘΕΟΣ ΕΥΠΑΤΩΡ ΦΙΛΕΛΛΗΝ						
	ΒΑΣΙΛΕΥΩΝ ΒΑΣΙΛΕΩΝ ΑΡΣΑΚΗΣ ΕΥΠΑΤΩΡ ΔΙΚΑΙΟΣ ΕΠΙΦΑΝΗΣ ΦΙΛΕΛΛΗΝ						
Orodes I.	ΒΑΣΙΛΕΥΣ ΒΑΣΙΛΕΩΝ ΜΕΓΑΣ ΑΡΣΑΚΗΣ ΚΑΙ ΚΤΙΣΤΗΣ						

Orodes I.	ΒΑΣΙΛΕΩΣ	ΒΑΣΙΛΕΩΝ	ΑΡΣΑΚΗΣ	ΦΙΛΟΠΑΤΩΡ	ΔΙΚΑΙΟΣ	ΕΠΙΦΑΝΗΣ	ΦΙΛΕΛΛΗΝ
	,,	,,	,,	,,	,,	,,	ΚΑΙ ΦΙΛΕΛΛΗΝ
	,,	,,	,,	ΕΥΕΡΓΕΤΗΣ	ΔΙΚΑΙΟΣ	ΕΠΙΦΑΝΗΣ	ΦΙΛΕΛΛΗΝ
	,,	,,	,,	ΔΙΚΑΙΟΣ			
	,,	,,	,,	ΦΙΛΕΛΛΗΝ			
	,,	,,	,,	ΟΡΩΔΗΣ			
Pacorus I.	ΑΡΣΑΚΗΣ	ΠΑΚΟΡΟΣ					
	ΒΑΣΙΛΕΥΣ	ΒΑΣΙΛΕΩΝ	ΑΡΣΑΚΗΣ	ΕΥΕΡΓΕΤΗΣ	ΔΙΚΑΙΟΣ	ΕΠΙΦΑΝΗΣ	ΦΙΛΕΛΛΗΝ
Phraates IV.	,,	,,	,,	,,	,,	,,	,,
	,,	,,	,,	,,	ΑΥΤΟΚΡΑΤΩΡ	ΕΠΙΦΑΝΗΣ	ΦΙΛΕΛΛΗΝ
Tiridates II.	,,	,,	,,	,,	ΔΙΚΑΙΟΣ	ΕΠΙΦΑΝΗΣ	ΦΙΛΕΛΛΗΝ
Phraataces	,,	,,	,,	,,	,,	,,	,,
	,,	,,					
Musa	ΘΕΑ	ΟΥΡΑΝΙΑ	ΜΟΥΣΗ	ΒΑΣΙΛΙΣΣΗ			
Sanabares	ΒΑΣΙΛΕΥΣ	ΜΕΓΑΣ	ΣΑΝΑΒΑΡΗΣ				
Orodes II.	ΒΑΣΙΛΕΥΣ	ΒΑΣΙΛΕΩΝ	ΑΡΣΑΚΗΣ	ΕΥΕΡΓΕΤΗΣ	ΔΙΚΑΙΟΣ	ΕΠΙΦΑΝΗΣ	ΦΙΛΕΛΛΗΝ
Vonones I.	,,	,,	,,	,,	,,	,,	,,
	,,	,,	ΟΝΩΝΗΣ				
	ΒΑΣΙΛΕΩΣ	ΟΝΩΝΗΣ	ΝΕΙΚΗΣΑΣ	ΑΡΤΑΒΑΝΟΝ			
Artabanus III.	ΒΑΣΙΛΕΥΣ	ΒΑΣΙΛΕΩΝ	ΕΥΕΡΓΕΤΗΣ	ΑΡΣΑΚΗΣ			
	,,	,,	ΔΙΚΑΙΟΣ	ΕΠΙΦΑΝΗΣ		.	
	,,	,,	ΑΡΣΑΚΗΣ	ΕΥΕΡΓΕΤΗΣ	ΔΙΚΑΙΟΣ	ΕΠΙΦΑΝΗΣ	ΦΙΛΕΛΛΗΝ
Vardanes I.	,,	,,	,,	,,	,,	,,	,,
Gotarzes	,,	,,	,,	,,	,,	,,	,,
	,, .	,,	,,	,,	,,	,,	ΓΩΤΑΡΖΗΣ
	ΓΩΤΕΡΖΗΣ	ΒΑΣΙΛΕΥΣ	ΒΑΣΙΛΕΩΝ	ΑΡΣΑΚΟΥ	ΥΟΣ ΚΕΚΑΛΟΥΜΕΝΟΣ	ΑΡΤΑΒΑΝΟΥ	
Vologeses I.	ΒΑΣΙΛΕΥΣ	ΒΑΣΙΛΕΩΝ	ΑΡΣΑΚΗΣ	ΕΥΕΡΓΕΤΗΣ	ΔΙΚΑΙΟΣ	ΕΠΙΦΑΝΗΣ	ΦΙΛΕΛΛΗΝ
Vardanes II.	,,	,,	,,	,,	,,	,,	,,
Vologeses II.	,,	,,	,,	,,	,,	,,	,,
Pacorus II.	,,	,,	,,	ΠΑΚΟΡΟΣ	,,	,,	,,
Artabanus IV.	,,	,,	,,	ΑΡΤΑΒΑΝΟΣ	,,	,,	,,
Vologeses III.	,,	,,	,,	ΟΛΑΓΑΣΗΣ	,,	,,	,,
Vologeses IV.	,,	,,	,,	,,	,,	,,	,,
Vologeses V.	,,	,,	,,	,,	,,	,,	,,
Vologeses VI.	,,	,,	,,	,,	,,	,,	,,

The King's name in Pehlvi characters is found on the coins of Mithradates IV., Vologeses IV., V., VI., Artabanus V., Artavasdes.

TABLE III.

PROBABLE SOURCE OF PARTHIAN TITLES.

TITLE.	KING.	SOURCE.
ΒΑΣΙΛΕΥΣ ΜΕΓΑΣ	Tiridates I. seqq.	Achæmenian Kings of Persia.
ΒΑΣΙΛΕΥΣ ΒΑΣΙΛΕΩΝ	Mithradates I., III., etc.	,, ,, ,,
ΦΙΛΑΔΕΛΦΟΣ	Phraapates	Ptolemy II. of Egypt.
ΦΙΛΕΛΛΗΝ	Phraapates seqq.	
ΘΕΟΠΑΤΩΡ	Phraates I., II.	
ΕΠΙΦΑΝΗΣ	Mithradates I. seqq.	Antiochus IV. of Syria.
ΔΙΚΑΙΟΣ	,, ,,	Agathocles of Bactria.
ΕΥΕΡΓΕΤΗΣ	Phraates II., Mithradates II., &c.	Antiochus VII. of Syria.
ΝΙΚΑΤΩΡ	Artabanus II.	Demetrius II. of Syria.
ΑΥΤΟΚΡΑΤΩΡ	Sinatroces, Phraates IV.	Sulla of Rome.
ΦΙΛΟΠΑΤΩΡ	Sinatroces seqq.	Antiochus IX. and foll. Kings of Syria.
ΕΥΠΑΤΩΡ	Mithradates III.	Mithradates VI. of Pontus.
ΚΤΙΣΤΗΣ	Orodes I.	Cities of Asia Minor.
ΘΕΑ ΟΥΡΑΝΙΑ	Musa	Cleopatra VI. of Egypt (ΘΕΑ ΝΕΩΤΕΡΑ).

*** It will be seen that the arrangement adopted in this paper is strongly corroborated by the facts collected in this table, whence it appears that in almost every case the Parthian King whom I suppose to have introduced a fresh title may have borrowed that title from a contemporary or slightly older ruler of some neighbouring country.

CORRIGENDA.

PAGE
7 line 24 *for* Atropatane *read* Atropatene.
12 at foot *transpose* notes 2 and 3.
16 line 31 *for* Artabanus IV. *read* Artabanus V.
17 line 10 *for* and the name of Artavasdes *read* and drachms bearing the name of Artavasdes.
25 at bottom *for* letter ⅄ *read* Σ.
49 line 36 *before* ΥΟΣ *insert* ΑΡΣΑΚΟΥ, cf. Table II.
62 ,,   6 *for* 310 Gor. *read* 310 Art.
64 lines 1 and 19 *for* ΒΑΣΙΛΕΩΣ *read* ΒΑΣΙΛΕΥΣ.

HERTFORD :
PRINTED BY STEPHEN AUSTIN AND SONS.

THE INTERNATIONAL NUMISMATA ORIENTALIA.

ADVANCED NOTICE.

Since the issue of the tentative prospectus of an International Numismata Orientalia, based upon the original edition of Marsden's Numismata Orientalia, some important modifications of the preliminary plan and general scope of the work have recommended themselves to the Publishers, which have equally commended themselves to the Editor's chief supporters.

The first design comprehended the narrow purpose of the continuation and completion of the substance of the old text published in 1822, with the concurrent reproduction of the admirably executed Copper-plates, prepared for Marsden's work, which had recently become the property of Messrs. Trübner & Co.

In both these departments the present undertaking now assumes a new and independent form. In lieu of accepting the task of making coins follow and supplement history, it seeks to prove the claims of Numismatic science to a higher mission in the illustration of the annals of olden time, to a power of instruction and teaching where written history is defective, and, in its lowest phase, of enabling us to test and rectify imperfectly preserved facts.

Under this expanded view, therefore, many subordinate sections of Marsden's old work will either be reduced to due proportions in reference to the uninstructive nature of their materials or omitted altogether: while on the other hand a class of subjects uncontemplated in the first International scheme will be introduced and included in this revised programme. For instance, instead of placing the Dynasties of the Khalifs of Baghdád, as of old, at the head of the list, a previous monograph has been devoted to the illustration of the first efforts in the art of coining, as exhibited in the electrum and gold pieces of Lydia and Persia, by Mr. Head. Mr. Gardner's contribution on the Parthians is now presented. These will be followed by the Phœnician coins of Asia Minor by our eminent German coadjutor, Dr. Euting; and Mr. Madden, whose specialité lies in the "History of the Jewish Coinages," will hereafter embody in our pages his exhaustive studies in that division of critical numismatics.

General Cunningham's Indo-Scythian series, the materials of which—enriched by the unprecedentedly valuable contents of the late Peshawar *find*—are arranged and on their way home from India—will now find a fitting introduction in a full and thrice-elaborated review of "the Bactrian successors of Alexander the Great," to which, as a labour of love, he has devoted himself since his first appearance as the chosen Numismatic coadjutor of James Prinsep in 1836.

Secondly, in regard to the illustrations of the old work, which it was once proposed to rely upon: they have been found, however excellent in themselves, practically unsuitable, either in grouping or mechanical accuracy, for the advanced demands of the present day. Indeed, the improved processes by which science has taught us to obtain, at a less cost, absolute *Sun* facsimiles, has necessarily superseded the hand and eye of the engraver, past or present, however perfect in his craft.

As far as the immediate state of the publication is concerned, it may be mentioned as a plea for seeming delay—that, in an amateur work of this kind, there are many obstacles to continuous or periodical issues, and it has been the Editor's aim rather to avoid such publications as were merely mechanical or repetitive; but, on the other hand, there has been no lack of support of the most efficient character, either at home or abroad — indeed, the Editor has had to decline many offers of contributions on the part of Numismatists of established reputation, as our lists are virtually made up beyond any prospect of absence of matter or immediate chance of publication of many of the already accepted papers.

Mr. Rhys Davids' Essay on Ceylon Coins only awaits the completion of the illustrations. Mr. Rogers' paper is ready and appears as Part IV. Sir W. Elliot and the Editor are engaged upon the Coins of Southern India— which have lately received some important accessions from Kolhápúr. M. Sauvaire's article has long been ready, under Mr. Rogers' careful translation, but its length has hitherto precluded its publication.

M. de Saulcy is, as of old, ever prepared to come to the front when his aid is called for,—and Dr. Blochmann has already done so much, in the Journal of the Asiatic Society of Bengal, towards the illustration of the local Coinages, that we have merely to reprint his papers whenever the serial arrangement of our articles may call for a consecutive continuation of the Pathán coins of Imperial Dehli. The Editor's own section of the general series is likewise reserved for somewhat similar motives.

M. Gregorieff's completion of his Tátar Dynasties has been deferred during his late duties as President of the Oriental Congress at St. Petersburg. M. Tiesenhausen, whom we might have enlisted and who would willingly join our ranks at this time, has anticipated us in his elaborate survey of "Les Monnaies des Khalifes Orientaux" (1873), which may well claim to constitute *the* standard authority, in its own department, for many years to come. In another division of Numismatics, the Russian savants have been in advance of us, in the publication of the plates of Sassanian coins representing the patient accumulations of 30 years of the life of M. de Bartholomæi (1873—second issue 1875, with an introduction by Prof. B. Dorn). These examples, however, prove less instructive than might have been anticipated. The sameness and iteration of the issues of the Sassanians has always been a subject of remark, but the singular deficiency of important novelties has seldom been so prominently displayed as in this collection, whose representative specimens spread over 32 well-filled 4to. plates.—[E. T.]

SUBJECTS ALREADY UNDERTAKEN, WITH THE NAMES OF CONTRIBUTORS.

Phœnician Coins	DR. JULIUS EUTING, Strassburg.
Coins of the Jews	MR. F. W. MADDEN.
Bactrian and Indo-Scythic Coins	GEN. A. CUNNINGHAM, Archæological Surveyor of India.
Coins of the Sassanians of Persia	MR. EDWARD THOMAS, F.R.S.
———— early Arabico-Byzantine adaptation . . .	M. F. DE SAULCY, Paris.
———— Southern India	SIR WALTER ELLIOT, late Madras C.S.
———— Ceylon	MR. RHYS DAVIDS, late Ceylon C.S.
———— Arakan and Pegu	SIR ARTHUR PHAYRE, late Commissioner of British Burmah.
———— the Khalifs of Spain, etc.	DON PASCUAL DE GAYANGOS, Madrid.
———— the Fatimites of Egypt	M. H. SAUVAIRE, Cairo.
———— the Ikhshídís	MR. REGINALD STUART POOLE, Keeper of Coins, B.M.
———— the Seljuks and Atábeks	MR. STANLEY L. POOLE, C.C.C., Oxford.
———— the Bengal Sultáns	DR. H. BLOCHMANN, Calcutta.
———— the Russo-Tátar Dynasties	PROFESSOR GREGORIEFF, St. Petersburg.

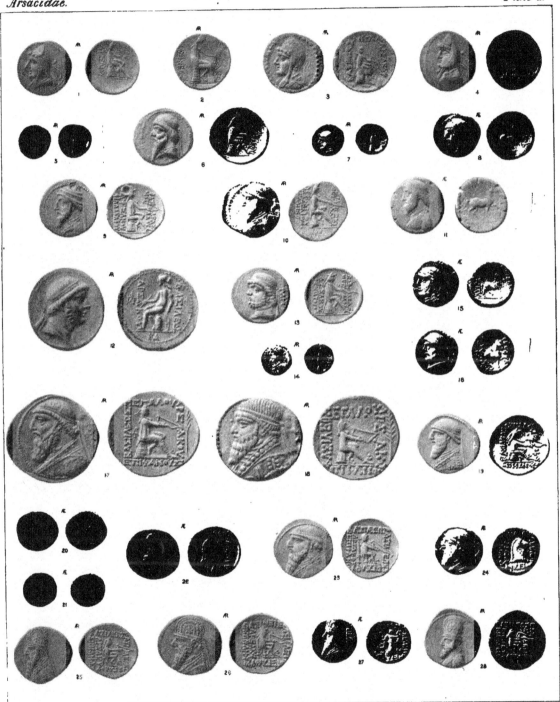

ARSACES I, TIRIDATES I, ARTABANUS I, PHRAAPATES, PHRAATES I,

MITHRADATES I.

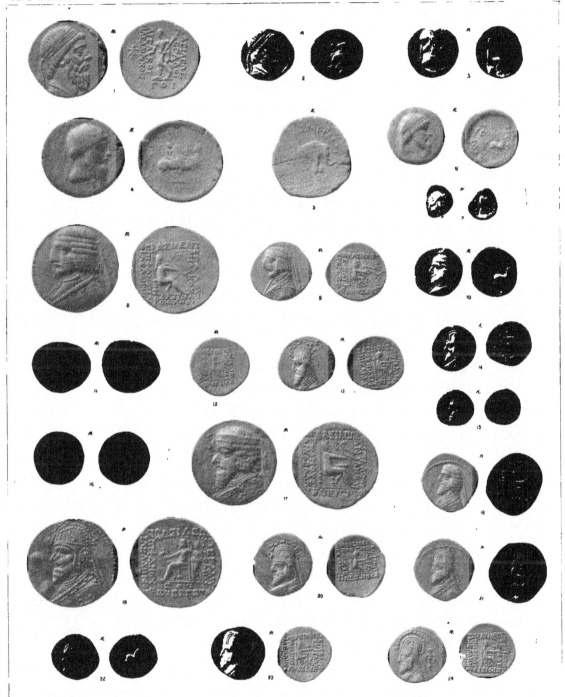

MITHRADATES I (SATRAPS,) PHRAATES II, ARTABANUS II, HIMERUS,
MITHRADATES II.

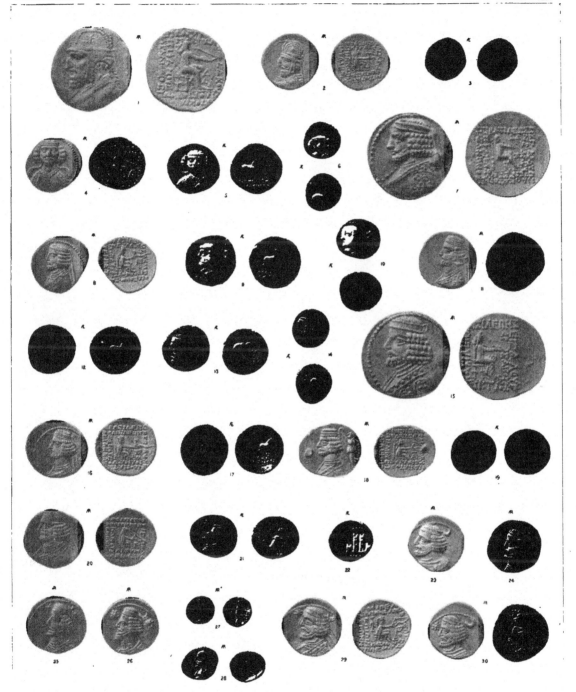

SINATROCES, PHRAATES III, MITHRADATES III, ORODES I.

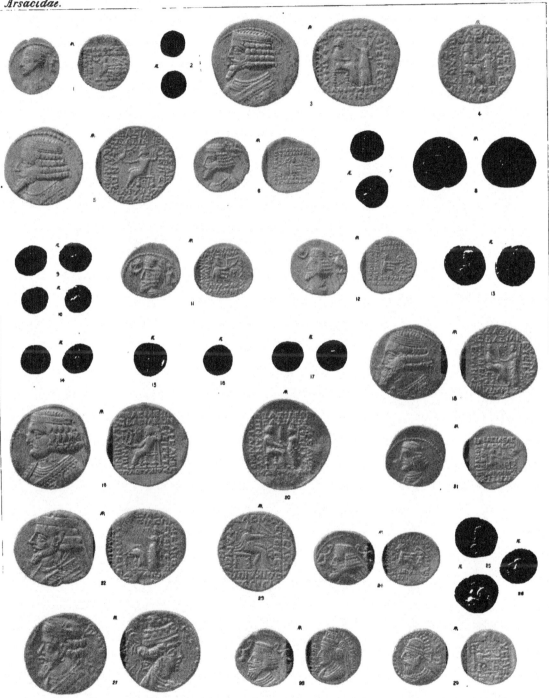

PACORUS, PHRAATES IV, TIRIDATES II, PHRAATACES, MUSA, SANABARES.

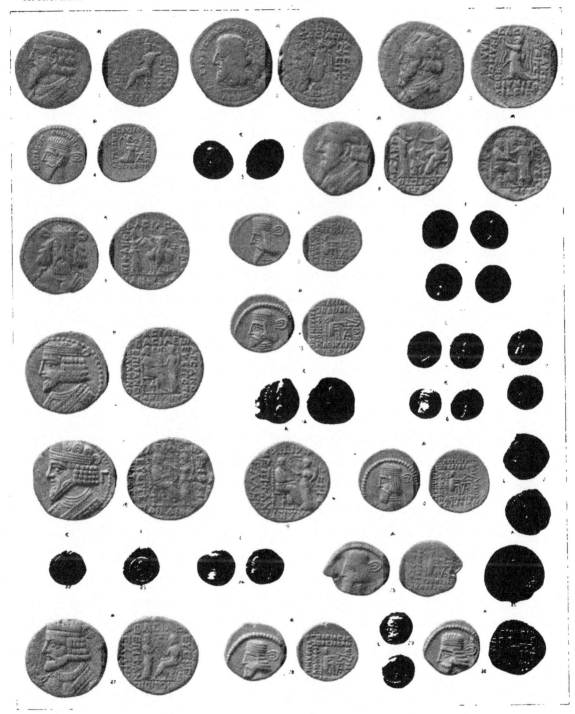

ORODES II, VONONES I, ARTABANUS III, VARDANES I, GOTARZES,
VOLOGESES I.

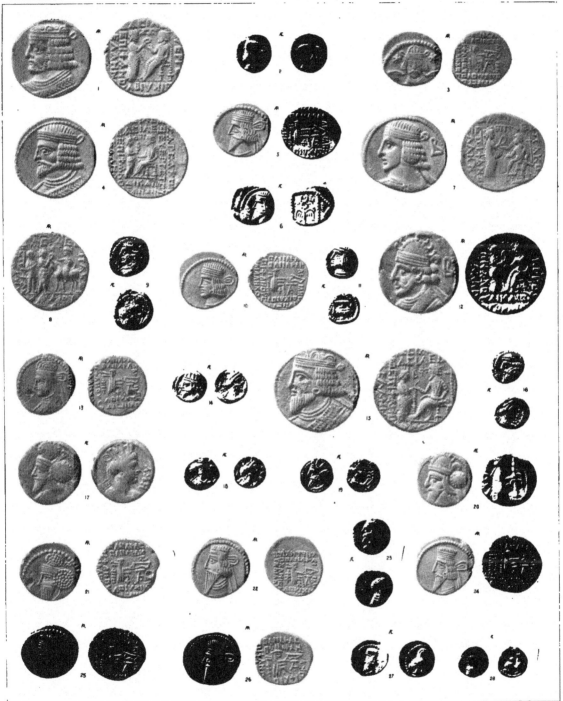

VARDANES II, VOLOGESES II. PACORUS II, ARTABANUS IV, CHOSROES,

MITHRADATES IIII

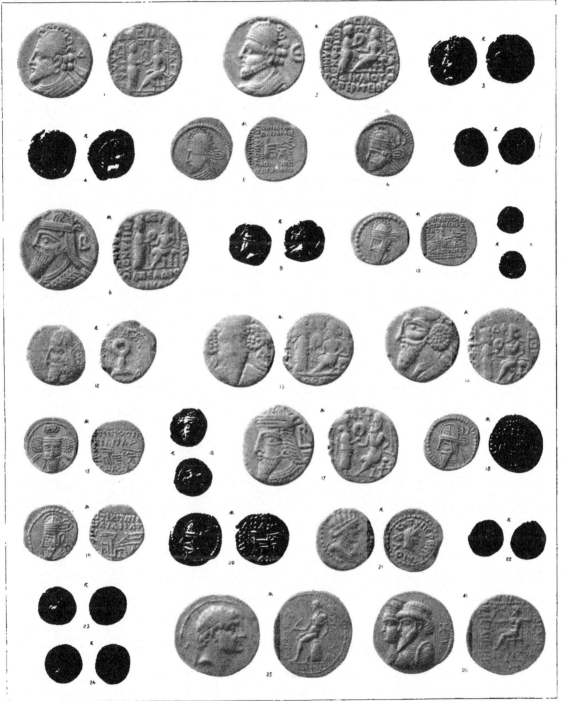

VOLOGESES III, IV, V, VI, ARTABANUS V, ARTAVASDES, CIVIC COINS,

KAMNASKIRES.

A ASSYRIAN HELMET.

B PARTHIAN HELMET.

C ROCK-SCULPTURE OF GOTERZES.

CPSIA information can be obtained
at www.ICGtesting.com
Printed in the USA
BVOW04s0857171116
468165BV00008B/55/P